*A Reporter Looks
at American Catholicism*

A Reporter Looks
at American Catholicism

by Barrett McGurn

CATHOLIC
PERSPECTIVES

General Editor: John J. Delaney

HAWTHORN BOOKS   *Publishers*   NEW YORK

First Edition: 1967

7740

To Jan and my mother
and
to Bill, Betsy, Andrew, Lachie and Martin

Contents

7

CONTENTS

Acknowledgments

A lifetime of friends and acquaintances are those whom I would like to thank for insights into the role of Catholicism now and in the future of our country. I would like to list a few.

The Reid family and John Hay Whitney as the owners of the New York *Herald Tribune* made possible three decades of reporting in twenty-five nations, but mostly in Rome and in New York. Wars, politics, crime, filled years of that news work, but from my first article for the *Herald Tribune* to my last on the final day of publication in April, 1966, a study of the Catholic Church in the world and in America ran as a persistent theme. As the *Tribune*'s "Catholic expert" over many years I saw Pius XII crowned as pontiff in 1939 and sealed in death in his triple casket in 1958. I saw John XXIII appear to the world as the new pope a few weeks later. I had off-the-record talks of a few minutes to as much as an hour and a quarter with each of the three recent popes, Pius XII, John XXIII and Paul VI, before or after they mounted Peter's throne.

The *Tribune* assignment opened doors and induced many confidences. For their help to my old paper and to me I wish

ACKNOWLEDGMENTS

to thank Cardinals Eugene Tisserant (the dean of the College of Cardinals who received all comers three times a week in his Vatican library office), Amleto Cicognani (Vatican State Secretary), Paul Emile Léger of Montreal, Richard Cushing of Boston, Francis J. Spellman of New York, Antonio Bacci, Peter Gregory XV Agagianian, Alfredo Ottaviani, Albert Gregory Meyer of Chicago, Valerio Valeri, Aloisius Muench, Elia Dalla Costa of Florence, J. Francis A. McIntyre of Los Angeles, Jozsef Mindszenty, Ernesto Ruffini, and Augustine Bea, all of whom in conversation or in correspondence fleshed out parts of my inquiry.

Many others should be listed: Archbishops Paul J. Hallinan of Atlanta and Martin J. O'Connor, who was then rector of the American seminary in Rome; Apostolic Delegate in America Egidio Vagnozzi and Apostolic Delegate in England Igino Cardinale; Bishops John J. Wright of Pittsburgh, Peter W. Bartholome of St. Cloud, Minnesota, and Ernest Primeau of New Hampshire; Father Robert Leiber, who was private secretary to Pius XII; Monsignors Alberto Giovanetti, the first full-time Vatican representative to the United Nations, and Timothy Flynn, the press spokesman for Cardinal Spellman; the late Father Vincent McCormick, who was the American representative in the world Jesuit leadership and rector of the Gregorian, Rome's main seminary; Father Roberto Tucci, editor of the ultra-papal *Civiltà Cattolica;* Father Francis Xavier Murphy (who always refused to concede that he was the main part of the brilliant Vaticanologist, Xavier Rynne); Monsignor Vincent A. Yzermans, the thoughtful, candid spokesman for the American hierarchy; Father Thurston Davis and all the priests at *America;* Father Ralph Gorman of *The Sign;* Monsignor John Tracy Ellis, the historian; Monsignor Richard H. J. Hanley of *The Long Island Catholic;* the late Father John La Farge; Monsignor Francis J. Lally of *The Pilot* of Boston; Father Gommar De Pauw of the "Catholic Traditionalists"; and the late heroic

Monsignor Hugh O'Flaherty of the Vatican Holy Office.

The list of laymen, too, is very long: discreet, helpful Count Enrico Galeazzi, governor of the Vatican State; Raimondo Manzini and Federico Alessandrini, editors of the Vatican daily *L'Osservatore Romano;* Luciano Casimirri, press officer of the Vatican; Martin H. Work, executive director of the American National Council of Catholic Men; Bob Hoyt of *The National Catholic Reporter;* Eileen Schaeffler of the *Grail;* the Pat Crowleys of the Christian Family Movement; Edward Simeon Skillin and John Leo of *Commonweal;* John F. Donnelly, president of the NCCM; Edward M. Keating of *Ramparts;* Gerard Sherry, of the Atlanta diocesan *Bulletin;* John O'Connor of the *Delmarva Dialogue;* James Norris, the first American layman to speak at an ecumenical council; Ed Wakin and Father Joseph F. Scheuer, Fordham faculty members and authors of *The De-Romanization of the American Catholic Church;* Dr. George Shuster of Notre Dame; Douglas Roche of *The Western Catholic Reporter* of Canada; and John J. Delaney, general editor of volumes in the Catholic Perspective series, and founder of "The Keys," a small, all but unknown New York Catholic discussion group which is sure to play a notable part in the American Catholic evolution.

To the Dominican sisters at St. Patrick's grammar school, to the Xaverian brothers at the now dissolved St. Michael's diocesan high school of Brooklyn, and to the Jesuit fathers of Fordham, I owe major appreciation for introducing me to ponderings which have gone on now for more than four decades. And to the staffs of the National Catholic Welfare Conference News Service, the Religious News Service, *Commonweal, ACT* of the Christian Family Movement, and many others, I wish to express special thanks for the reporting they have done, making it possible to piece together this picture of an important transitional moment in the story of America and of Catholicism. The responsibility for inter-

11

pretations and conclusions is my own. They do not necessarily represent the opinion of the various kind persons who have contributed large or small pieces to the working out of the puzzle.

Foreword

This book is a sequel to one published five years ago, *A Reporter Looks at the Vatican.*

The first was the fruit of thirteen years in Rome as bureau chief for a great, liberal American newspaper, the New York *Herald Tribune,* which has now unhappily closed its doors after a radiant 131-year history. I saw Rome professionally as a newsman and personally as an American and as a Catholic. I sought to report on the world headquarters of the Catholic Church with unsparing objectivity, yet with sympathy.

The aim of the Vatican book was to answer whether the anachronistic and, in many ways, premedieval papal court continues as a significant force in a century in which one "Saturday religion page" satisfies the church-news needs of most dailies. My answer was that the Vatican, with all its provincialisms, all the petty human failings, all the paraphernalia of earlier and surpassed eras, was indeed a clear and loud page-one voice for values which this century can ill afford to forget.

This volume attempts to do something similar for the writer's fellow Catholics of the United States, a group I began covering for the *Herald Tribune* before World War

II, and among whom I have always lived. Each book has tried to present a realistic portrait from within, outlining weaknesses, shortcomings, lapses, the superstition, the betrayal of ideals, the excesses, along with reasons for approval and for hope. This volume sets itself several goals: to discuss whether there is any real place for Catholicism or any other religion in an America of expanding educational and scientific achievements, or whether, in fact, the very accomplishments of the United States have accentuated the religious needs of a successful, gayly entertained and often weary population; to outline the gap between the world vision of popes such as John XXIII and Paul VI and the mean anti-Semitism, racism, isolation and bigotry of so many American Catholic rightists; to portray some of the history which has led laymen to be pope-makers in some centuries and mute men in parish pews in recent generations; to talk of the education explosion and the hopes for a significant American Catholic contribution to United States culture; and to report on some of the ferments of change which have reached into cloistered convents, into Middle Western college campuses, into seminaries and rectories, into Holy Name Societies and Knights of Columbus councils, into bishops' residences and, indeed, into every corner of American Catholic life.

There are paradoxes and contradictions, but there is sure evidence that the "moment's inspiration," as jolly, obese John XXIII called it in 1959, has changed your American Catholic neighbor forever. A new free spirit, fanned by the ecumenical council which was John's "inspiration," is at work in every Catholic schoolroom and inside every Catholic family. The American Catholic giant is awakening. Will that mean the birth of a new political movement, modeled perhaps after the Christian Democratic parties which took power under Italy's Alcide De Gasperi, France's Robert Schuman and West Germany's Konrad Adenauer following World War II? Will this be a responsible, constructive force to add a new spiritual dimension to United States life, or will it follow the essentially negative pattern of American Catholic film censorship groups, "clean book" campaigns and similar gestures of a largely defensive immigrant past? Will American laymen such as James Norris of Rumson, New Jersey, join the elegant knee-breeched Italian noblemen at the papal court, but as social workers with a modern vision and administrative power, not as mere additions to the quaint, empty trappings of a closed clerical past? To each of these the book proposes answers.

The long dormant Catholic one-quarter of America is emerging from a sleep tracing back to the Revolutionary War era when political limitations against Catholics slowly were lifted inside the various colonies. This is a fact of importance to all Americans. An aggressive, confident, repressive Catholic force—and there are those American Catholics who would like to see its birth—would be an important new ally for the conservative wing of the political spectrum. An educated, dedicated Catholic consensus fostered by the world-aid dreams of John XXIII would, on the other hand, be a help to those who advocate a generous foreign assistance program. Politicians who once counted on Catholic bloc votes in New York, Boston, Chicago and the other great cities would do well to study the changing American Catholic layman, for his convictions, his loyalties and his numbers will tip the balance in hundreds of municipal, congressional and perhaps even presidential elections.

The new American Catholic I envisage will be less and less a mass voter, less and less a sure thing for politicians who think that a ticket of an Irishman or Italian Holy Name member, plus a Negro and a Jew, is the formula for victory in big cities. More and more he will reflect the first American Catholic president, who had this conversation, as reported to the writer by an onlooker:

Visitor: "Mr. President, you should do something for so-and-so. He's a Catholic, you know."

President Kennedy: "So-and-so? He's a Catholic? I didn't

know it. Well, no, he's fine where he is. That's where I want him."

John Fitzgerald Kennedy, a devout Catholic and a dedicated American liberal, was no bigot. Fellow Americans who fear the rise of an American Catholic power bloc endangering civil liberties may, in my opinion, put such fears to rest. There will be an awakened Catholic, summoned from a long slumber by sideless, brilliant Pope John. But more and more he will be a new man, confident on American soil, aware of his share in the fight for United States freedoms and civic progress, and self-assured, too, in preaching American democratic ideals inside the papal court in Rome.

The new American Catholic layman, like John F. Kennedy, his finest prototype, will be a man who will rely more heavily on his own conscience, aware that he must be a self-starter and self-reliant in translating noble principles of his faith into concrete contributions to the American community. An excessively clerical era is ending. For clergy this will mean painful readjustments and for laymen a unique era. Because of the great share of Catholic Church responsibilities sure to shift to the laymen who make up 99 percent of the Catholic community, this volume concentrates especially on the laity, their mental make-up, their future. What follows is what this reporter sees midway in a lifelong look at his fellow fifty million American Catholics.

Barrett McGurn

New York
September 15, 1966

Part I

The Catholic Yesterday

ONE

Mute Man in the Pew

The tongue-tied layman in the pew, or even the lector who reads a few texts inside the altar rail of America's Catholic churches, is unrecognizable in terms of the early Christianity reflected amid the ruins of Rome.

Visit the catacombs of Priscilla under the wheels of the traffic on Via Salaria at the north edge of the Eternal City. Deep under the pavement you will find a room where the Mass must have been recited in the early decades of the Church. The chamber, carved from rock, is cramped. The priest who prayed there was part of a tiny congregation. He could not have been far from the laymen in whatever sense, physically, spiritually, or even in an understanding of the simple lessons of the generous new philosophy which had taken root in the cruel, blood-greedy, indolent soil of a dying empire.

Nor could the reading of the Gospels have suggested a gulf between clerics and laity. Christ after all had preached against a formalistic, dessicated clergy. He Himself was only a carpenter—a layman in the old religion, though the God-priest of the new. The apostles were laymen—fishermen, a tax collector, though transformed by Christ's order and by

Divine inspiration into teachers, interpreters and "bishops" of the new faith. The Acts of the Apostles record one of the first labors of Jesus' emissaries: the organization of an order of deacons, men of a lesser church rank, to wait on table and to handle other mundane tasks. From the earliest moments there were needed, useful, active roles alongside and in addition to the central and essential one of the clergy.

There is debate among archaeologists in Rome about whether many Christians died in the savage spectacles inside the hulking Colosseum, but there is little question that many were slain a few hundred feet away along another of the modern Italian capital's automobile raceways. The other site is a two-square-block area in a hollow at the foot of the abrupt Palatine Hill, the mound on which the emperors lived (a fact which gave the word "palace" to Western languages). That is where chariots spun around the track of the Circus Maximus. It is a bare, weedy area now with hardly a rubble pile to suggest what used to be there. But no doubt exists that Christians by scores, priest and laymen alike, died together at the spot, guaranteeing that their faith would become a dominant world force for millennia.

Rome's stones and murals tell the story over and over again. Midway between the Colosseum and the Circus Maximus is a rococo church perched opposite the Palatine on the Caelian, another of Rome's seven hills. It is called the Church of Sts. John and Paul. The Passionist order has its generalate in the old monastery next door. Inside the monks' gardens are the sluices through which water was poured into the Colosseum for naval battles during the ferocious first century of the Christian era. About the time of World War I a monk at Sts. John and Paul was troubled by the fashion of the times to doubt much of Christian lore as faulty fancy, as mistold legends which, in many cases, lacked basis in fact. The monk fell ill. He promised in prayers that if he recovered he would set out to prove that there had been two saints, John and Paul, that they had lived about A.D. 300,

20

that they were officers of the emperor, and that they had died rather than renounce the young and unaccepted religion of Christ. The priest got well. He opened a hole in the church pavement and underneath, after months of excavating, found a third-century Roman house which showed every sign that it had been a pagan dwelling and that it had been turned into a make-do Christian church. A fairly well-done nude mural in a room under the church's high altar had been whitewashed over some sixteen centuries ago. In the next room was a mural of a woman in long dress, her arms raised as if in adoration—evidently an "orante," a symbol of prayer. Down in the foundations there was a pit around which ancient frescoes told the story of a decapitation. In a widely accepted interpretation, that is where executed occupants of the house were buried, and where fellow Christians came to pray—the beginning of a cult which 1,600 years later is still conserved by the monks of the monastery next door.

Priests and people were slain for the faith side by side and separately. No closer bond was possible. Yet at the two-thirds mark of the twentieth century a humorous, quietly aggressive American bishop, Ernest A. Primeau, of New Hampshire, told ecumenical council fathers in Rome that the layman of Catholicism had been reduced merely to "believe, pay, pray and obey."

What caused the change?

The American National Council of Catholic Men in 1963 produced a youth training film series making the point that the barbarian invasions during the fourth century, during the very first decades of legal Christianity, had scooped hordes of near savages into the Christian faith. Theirs was an act of will but scarcely one of an informed intellect. More than the Mysteries were mysteries to them, and the priest took on an expanded responsibility for guidance and decision. The mute man of the twentieth-century pew had a forerunner.

If indeed the silence of the layman goes back so far in

21

Church history there is no doubt that succeeding centuries saw laymen in Church roles of utmost significance. Some, women as well as men, made eminent contributions as saints, martyrs, students, social reformers, seers. The pages of ecclesiastical history are bright with the names of many: the mother of St. Augustine, Monica, herself a saint; the witty, cultured, beheaded hero, St. Thomas More; Pauline Jericot, the Frenchwoman who begged for the Catholic missions and created a Vatican Congregation (for the Propagation of the Faith) ; Frederic Ozanam, the Sorbonne professor who founded the Society of St. Vincent de Paul in Paris in 1833— the list, happily, is lengthy. Even in our own century the parade has been a crowded one, many of its members statesmen such as America's first Catholic President, JFK, a man whose Catholic faith infused his Harvard culture; France's Robert Schuman ("father of united postwar Europe") ; Germany's postwar Chancellor Konrad Adenauer; Italy's postfascist premier, lean, gentle, great-souled Alcide De Gasperi; France's philosopher Jacques Maritain and armies of others.

That was one side of lay activity. There was another, too, as *The Popes,*[1] edited by Eric John, pointed out.

The awe of the fourth century, when barbarian laymen listened silently to the good news of the priests, did not endure for many generations. By the latter part of the first millennium laymen owned hereditary rights to many church benefices. Priests, bishops, abbots regularly paid for office. It took two hundred years for the reforming monks of Cluny in France and for popes of the stamp of Leo IX (1049–1054) to strike down lay-exploited simony.

For centuries around the turn of the millennium laymen had a strong say in papal elections. Sometimes one layman controlled papal designations for several pontificates in a row. The infamous Marozia, a central figure in Rome society in the tenth century, looked on in A.D. 904 as her parents maneuvered Sergius III onto the papal throne. The evidence is that she had a son by this pontiff. The child was the same one Marozia later installed in Peter's chair to serve from 931 to 935 or 936. In between, one or more of the popes benefited from Marozia's conniving. Marriage to her brother-in-law, an incestuous arrangement in the view of the Roman population, finally brought on Marozia's imprisonment. She disappeared from history's pages even though her son, the pope, had given her the marriage dispensation she had wished and had presided at her wedding.

From 973 to 1009 the Crescentius family of Rome, who seem to have been relatives of Marozia, dictated the election of one pope after another. With the death of John Crescentius in 1012 a brighter day in papal history dawned, but even as late as the sixteenth century cardinals were unnerved by Roman mobs shouting protests when the official papal electors dared to choose a non-Roman. In 1939 this writer heard the dim echoes of that Roman spirit when Eugenio Pacelli became Pius XII. Although the austere churchman had no doubt about the fulness of clerical responsibility inside pope-electing conclaves, there was nothing he could do to restrain the mass of nearly half a million inside the colonnades facing St. Peter's Basilica. There was an almost tangible emotion as the throng waited for the name of the new pope, "His eminence, Eugene . . ." That was all that was needed. There were two Eugenes in the College of Cardinals, the other a multilingual boy wonder of the French church and of the Vatican, Cardinal Tisserant, but the Romans took the view that the selection of a non-Italian was unthinkable. There was only one Italian "Eugene" and he was Roman-born. That was what the mob wanted. Their cry of joy made clear how disappointed they would have been had a non-Roman been chosen. It was no business of the crowd to make decisions about such matters but it did, and the cardinals assuredly got the message: "We Romans are glad that, for the first time in several pontificates, you

have picked a Roman; we Italians want you to go on in the
future picking Italians." It is a long time since many have
given thought to Marozia and the Crescentius family of
Rome, but the diplomats who conversed with the cardinals
at the time of the election of Pope John XXIII (a north
Italian) told me, "Since Italians are so anxious to have an
Italian, and since the papacy is in Rome, it seems best to go
along with it."

That such an arbitrary limitation on the choice open to
cardinals might bring a lesser man to Peter's throne was
evident, but the lay mob, as so often in the past, had its
effect.

Perhaps more astonishing than the simoniacal lay control
of benefices in Christianity's middle years and the recurrent
lay intrusion in papal elections is the fact that laymen have
more than once occupied the chair of Christ's Vicar. Eric
John's *The Popes,* again, tells the story strikingly. Fabian
happened to be an onlooker at the time of the election in
236. He was an out-of-towner unknown to the voters, but a
dove settled on his head. This was taken as a sign, according
to Eusebius. Fabian was chosen, serving as pope until 250. In
963 a layman was elected pontiff as Leo VIII. A functionary
of the papal court, he had conducted negotiations with
Emperor Otto I, who had taken a liking to him. A council
summoned by the emperor deposed the reigning pope, John
XII, but the idea of a layman being elected pontiff was so
shocking to medieval Europe that Leo ruled only fitfully for
two years and is omitted from the Vatican list of true popes.

Yet worse in the tangled story which is papal history is,
parenthetically, the memory of those few popes who acted
like the least spiritual of laymen. One was the John XII who
was overthrown to make way for the layman Leo VIII. John
preferred hunting to church ceremonies, and served from 955
to 964 (overlapping briefly with Leo VIII). A century later
Benedict IX virtually relived the story of John XII. In his

case it was his predecessor rather than his successor who was a layman, Senator Romanus, who frankly purchased his election. Romanus served from 1024 to 1032 as John XIX. *The Popes* sums him up tersely: "young, wholly secular in his outlook, immoral, cruel and indifferent to spiritual things—the testimony to his depravity is disinterested and overwhelming."

Uncles and aunts of the Tusculani family had obtained Peter's throne for Benedict IX. He lived with the mockery of his position for some years and then grew "tired . . . and wished to marry and settle down." He arranged for a successor who agreed to pension him. The new pope was the otherwise virtuous John Gratian (Pope Gregory VI, 1045–1046). The ex-Benedict IX survived to see four others on his abandoned throne.

Laymen selling church offices, laymen naming popes, popes emulating the least spiritual of the laity—this was one of the many low points in the story of the Christian faith and, providentially, all this was corrected or, less fortunately, overcorrected. The declining days of the Middle Ages set the stage of Church history for another drama, the Protestant Reformation and the stern Counter-Reformation. Four centuries later every Christian lives with the tumultuous consequences of that sixteenth-century explosion.

The rights of nations and indeed the privileges of the ever more literate laymen were values dear to many of the reformers. The ideal of Rome-centered unity was equally clear to the fathers of the Trent ecumenical council. Battle lines were drawn and truths or partial truths fell on both sides of the front as Christianity slid into civil war. A bitter heritage has been the lot of all Christians, clergy and laity alike, Catholic and Protestant, ever since, for Protestants have been frustrated in the search for a world faith which is the logical quest of each believing person, and Catholics have been trapped into anti-intellectual and often narrowly Italian positions which bear scant resemblance to the open, all-encompassing faith of Christianity's infant years.

In the first decades of this century it was the custom in American Catholic colleges to heap coals on the heads of the Protestant reformers and to tell, as cheerfully as facts would allow, the story of four hundred years of rear-guard actions leading to the fortress church symbolized by the papal prisoner in the Vatican Palace of 1870 to 1929. That, at least, is how my Fordham University (New York) religion courses seemed to me. But there are new evaluations now. As Father George H. Tavard, a member of the American bishops' press panel at the ecumenical council, commented in a National Catholic Welfare Conference article in the fall of 1964:

Since the sixteenth century, ecclesiology, or reflection on the Church, has gone in the one-sided direction of self-defense against the real or imaginary assaults of Protestants, Deists, rationalists, modernists, materialists and atheists.

This did strengthen the Church's interior discipline and coherence, but it also hastened her loss of contact with the masses of many countries and with the intellectual concerns of the educated.

The institution of the Church and its hierarchy came out of this immeasurably more powerful than before in their narrow confines, yet considerably weakened in their impact on society and on the shape of modern thought. As a result the Church became increasingly irrelevant to the concrete problems of men. It is this fatal trend that Pope John XXIII wanted to stop by calling a council for a profound renovation of the Church.

Christopher Dawson in *Progress and Religion*[2] insists that modern criticism of great religions in general must be accepted as valid to a degree:

Their [the religions'] intellectual absolutism and their concentration on metaphysical conceptions have tended to turn men's minds away from the material world, and from practical social activity. But this preoccupation with the eternal and the Absolute and the spirit of "other worldliness" which it generates is anti-

26

pathetic to the modern mind, since it seems ultimately to destroy
the value and the signification of relative knowledge, that is to
say of natural science, and of human life itself.

The present age seems to demand a religion which will be an
incentive to action and a justification of the material and social
progress which has been the peculiar achievement of the last two
centuries.

If the charge of gathering irrelevance in the recent centuries of education, industry and science is to be leveled
against all religions, surely it must be conceded that the
Protestant areas of northern Europe and the largely Protestant United States have been immeasurably more successful
in unleashing productive, scholarly and even civic energies
during the generations since Luther. By the sheer arith-
metic of those involved, these were largely lay energies.
Europe's Catholic countries—Italy, Spain, Portugal, Ireland,
France in a sense—and Latin America conserved many of the
forms of the ancient faith, but any American traveling in
those lands is dismayed by a brooding somnolence and by the
conscienceless gulf between rich and poor. Clerical dominance inside the Church has been all but total, and many of
the most unselfish and sublime instincts of the laymen, who
are the overwhelming majority of Church membership, have
gone unused. Where there is no immediate responsibility
there is little challenge.

Father John B. Sheerin, editor of *The Catholic World,* the
New York Paulist monthly, traces the stultification of so
much of the modern Catholic contribution to a period some
time after the Council of Trent. Father Sheerin said in an
editorial in July, 1964:

The Tridentine spirit was a creative one, religiously, artistically,
and even politically. But today's Catholic ultra-conservatism is
narrow-minded, critical, defensive, an attitude of mind that takes
its rise in the last century in Italy.

When the pope became the prisoner of the Vatican, the Catholic

27

response to the Risorgimento was a living protest against liberalism. Catholic Rome retreated into clericalism, isolating itself from the contemporary world and striving to turn the hands of the clock back to the past. Our Catholic life since, according to Purdy,[3] has reflected this siege mentality and anticulture.

When Pope Paul (as Father Montini) began his post-graduate course at Rome he enrolled for a course in Italian literature but his Roman mentors told him he would be wasting his time. . . . I remember hearing of an old Roman ecclesiastic who commented on some of the theology of Germans at the council, "the old miasma comes once again over the Alps." Romanità is a super-orthodoxy that does not hesitate to look with suspicion even on Bishops of great learning and integrity, if they come from outside Rome.

Father Sheerin's point was that the Catholic Church of the final years of the twentieth century had to distinguish "what is Roman from what is Catholic."

To be merely Roman and specifically Roman clerical would be indeed a tragic end for the inspiration which sank stout roots in Rome nineteen centuries earlier. Yet there were many reasons to fear that the Catholic Church prior to Pope John XXIII had become merely Roman clerical, as this writer found in thirteen years of life in Rome (from 1946 to 1952 and from 1955 to 1962). G. Naidenoff, S.J., in *The Catholic Church in World Affairs*[4] appropriately pointed out that these were the nationalities of the saints canonized in the nineteenth and early twentieth centuries: Austrian, 1; German, 1; Spanish, 5; French, 19; Italian, 29; The United States and the 100 other nationalities, none.

That little Italy with 2 percent of the world's population, 6 percent of the Christians of the planet and a tenth of the Catholics had more than half the sanctity was, of course, absurd. Yet to the Roman clerical mind it was by no means so ridiculous. The widespread feeling in the Rome of the nineteen-forties and -fifties was that "universal" and "Roman" were synonymous. To the archly conservative

Roman mentality Paris, London, Bonn, Moscow, New York and Washington were the provinces. That surely was true when Christianity was born. It certainly was false in a scientific century which had left modern Rome in its backwaters.

Even more distressing was that papal Rome in the mid-twentieth century was only a sliver even of Rome itself, just as Catholic Italy was only a narrow slice of a nation of fifty million inhabitants. At the time of the conclaves in 1939 and in 1958 when Pius XII and John XXIII were elected to Peter's throne there was every indication that the Italian share of the College of Cardinals (two thirds in 1939, one third in 1958) prided itself on the quasi-governmental status of Catholicism in Italy (the one official state religion). No cardinals from the Protestant north of Europe or from the United States could vaunt anything similar. All but a handful of Italians were listed as Catholics. Yet an Irish-American Catholic from New York felt himself among religious strangers in most Italian groups. Whether among the buxom bikini-clad, long-tressed girls of the Riviera beaches, whether at showings of films with Communist overtones, whether scanning the columns of agnostic newspapers or whether listening to any of a thousand conversations at parties, in trains, in clubs or anywhere else inside the peninsula, the visitor found the average Italian "layman" as far removed from the Church and the Sunday Mass as the French anticlerical or the Protestant Northerner. If the faith of the past century has been Italian in its manifestations, it has been merely a remote clerical Italian, distant even from Italy, let alone from the average twentieth-century man.

The clerical Rome of the time before the daring John XXIII was a community locked off even from the city of two million Romans. At the parliament and at the receptions in the presidential palace where one met the leaders of the nation, Vatican figures rarely were seen. Severe rules, pre-

29

sumably designed in part to evade the taunts of the antireligious, kept the clergy out of the opera, out of the theaters, and off the streets in the evening. The bustling life of the downtown restaurants and hotels could be lived without reference to the presence in Rome of the world headquarters of the Church. When plans were made for the ecumenical council before 1962 I was told that the whole three thousand bishops of the Catholic world could assemble with scarcely a note taken of it in the broad spaces of the Italian capital.

At the highest places in the Vatican, siblings could be found occupying pinnacles. In my first years there were the two Archbishops Costantini, sons of a humble family. In my later years there were the two Cardinals Cicognani, also children of homes without special pretense. One of the Archbishops Costantini told me, as head of the Congregation for the Propagation of the Faith, how Catholicism might have to adapt rituals to the customs of Hindu India. Only someone such as he at highest church levels would handle such a matter. One of the Cardinals Cicognani was Secretary of State, number-two man of Catholicism, under Popes John XXIII and Paul VI. Visiting him I was startled to find a baseball in his official quarters, a humble and prized souvenir of his quarter of a century as the papal representative in Washington. I wondered often about the two sets of brother prelates, all from simple Italian homes, and all of them in positions of capital world Catholic influence. How else could such coincidences be explained except by the fact that Catholic leadership had shrunk into the narrow range of Italian clerical hands, thus making it possible for a very few families to provide the men who would give guidance to the whole of the modern Catholic world. Was one to believe that only Italy had the education, only Italy possessed the Divine grace, to give the 550 million Catholic laymen of the world their direction? I could not believe so.

30

This central Roman clerical world into which Catholic supremacy had devolved through the centuries was not without laymen, but there were few of them. Some presided at international conferences of the Catholic laity. There was Dr. Luigi Gedda, a physician, an expert on the subject of twins. He made the Catholic Action organization the main political force in Italy during the critical struggle with communism in 1948. I found him a dour and rather suspicious, monosyllabic man when I interviewed him as an American reporter. He preached a doctrine of state paternalism which, I thought, had overtones of the fascism of his childhood. At one of Pope John's first audiences I saw the place Dr. Gedda took, on one of the lower steps of the throne, not as high as the pontiff, but loftier than the rest of us. To me it was a symbol of a clericalism which is outside the experience either of Protestants or of Catholics of the United States and surely would trouble both of them. In following months, as Pope John pulled the Italian Catholic Church back from its deep involvement in national politics, Dr. Gedda's prominence faded.

Another of the laity prominent in the Rome of the nineteen forties and fifties was Dr. Riccardo Galeazzi-Lisi, an eye doctor who is said to have treated the future Pius XII for a cold one day when the latter visited him for new glasses. The oculist became the official papal physician and, indeed, the doctor of the 1,000-person Vatican State, one of the few who shared in the casual conversations of the lonely dedicated priest who was Pius XII. Then, with the help of another, at Pius's death, the eye specialist tried his hand at a new kind of embalming, a whole new area for him. The papal embalming publicly and scandalously went awry. The one great lay bubble which the eye doctor represented at the almost wholly clerical Vatican burst with a splash. The College of Cardinals, in charge during the papal interregnum, banned the oculist-embalmer from the Vatican State, and the Italian medical profession began disciplinary proceedings.

In an era when thousands of scientific laboratories and hundreds of publishing houses each year pushed back the frontiers of knowledge, at a time when the medieval monks' near-monopoly on learning had long since been surpassed, it was evident that the type of lay presence at the papal court represented by Dr. Galeazzi-Lisi or even by Dr. Gedda was grievously insufficient. Laymen leading in government, in science, in the arts, needed easier access to the churchmen who were making vastly influential moral judgments on volatile situations. Clerics required the facts which lay experts could give them, just as lay persons everywhere inevitably would be affected by positions taken by the papacy and by the world hierarchy on the legitimacy of wars, on the morality of escalation, on birth control, and on a hundred other subjects. As Dr. Galeazzi-Lisi's case in the late fifties emphasized, a historic gulf between clergy and laity was still broad, but its narrowing on all levels, at the Vatican, at Church national headquarters, in dioceses and in parishes, was imminent and inevitable and, in some cases, fortunately already begun.

two

American and Catholic

⤸

The parabola of the decline of the layman in the world Church has followed the same curve, in some ways a deeper one, inside the United States. The American Catholic Church at the start of the final third of the twentieth century finds itself the richest center of world Catholicism, not only in terms of bank accounts and physical investments, but also as a source of religious vocations. Yet the lay Catholic achievement in the United States in wedding Catholicism and Americanism has been so poor that the lay Catholic often is a split personality—a Catholic at Sunday Mass, an American during the rest of the week, two different people in each of the roles.

Catholic parish churches of America display the red, white and blue Old Glory and the white and yellow insignia of the Vatican State, but brooks of tears have been shed in the effort to bring the two banners together. Until the brief incumbency of John F. Kennedy, the martyr president of the early sixties, there were surely many who wondered secretly whether "the world" of so much of American life could be reconciled with the devotions practiced behind the walls of the parish church.

Only now in the wake of the revolution of the two Johns—President John Kennedy and Pope John XXIII—have many American Catholic laymen begun to feel at ease and at home inside their two societies.

The American Catholic layman has been well aware of his status as a member of a minority in a predominantly Protestant nation. The older he is, the more painful are his memories of an earlier day when Catholics were notably unwelcome in the land. Few are so young that they have not heard of the "wasp"—white Anglo-Saxon Protestant—tradition which is dominant. Most remember when the Ku Klux Klan was anti-Catholic as well as anti-Jewish and anti-Negro, an attitude which only now is beginning to change in heavily Catholic Northeastern areas where such men as Frank Rotella, the Italian-origin, Catholic-raised King Kleagle (organizer) of the New Jersey state Klan, begin to see Catholics as a pool from which Negro-haters and anti-Semites can be fished.

Among those in their fifties there is the recollection of the 1928 presidential campaign of gravel-tongued Alfred E. Smith, a social reformer with a great heart, but a New Yorker with a gutter diction offensive to the broad mass of Americans. Al Smith was fought as an opponent of Prohibition, but I remember my shock at fourteen when my well-meaning Protestant neighbor, an osteopath, assured me that the Catholic candidate was not only an opponent of the theory of the dry laws but also a helpless drunk who "just a few days ago needed a man on either side to hold him on his feet." Those were the days of the story that the pope in the Vatican would be the absentee master of the White House, and that a secret tunnel might be built to link the cellars of St. Peter's with the executive mansion at 1600 Pennsylvania Avenue.

A few American Catholics have known from parochial schooling that their faith has old roots in United States soil. Monsignor John Tracy Ellis, in his *American Catholicism*,[1] has listed some of them:

34

Catholic Spain ruled the American Southland for three centuries and has left a memento in names sprinkled across the map—St. Augustine, Florida (where the first American Catholic parish was established in 1565, fifty-five years before the Pilgrim landings) ; San Antonio, Texas; Los Angeles, San Francisco.

Catholic France explored the Middle West and left a similar legacy of place names—Marietta, Ohio (named for the ill-destined Marie Antoinette) , Vincennes, Dubuque, St. Louis (called after France's saint-king) and Louisville (honoring another of the Paris monarchs, Louis XVI) .

But if all that is true, a far more important influence in forming the mute man in the American Catholic twentieth-century pew was the England of King Henry VIII, the country of Cromwell, the England which broke from the Church of Rome during the century of the birth of the Protestant Reformation, the land which conquered Catholic Ireland, the nation which exported to America both the free spirit of the Magna Carta and also the tradition of a harsh Protestant-Catholic clash.

If England's memory of Henry VIII and of Cromwell faded and mellowed with the years, and if the American society evolved as it did away from the early oppressive anti-Catholic laws of the English colonies, vanquished Ireland and the Irish priests who soon dominated the Catholic hierarchy of the United States forgot very little. The two— Yankee nervousness about Catholics, and Catholic and especially Irish resentment over offenses of past and present— combined to produce the uneasy and often ineffectual Catholic layman of our time.

Bitter memories die slowly. An example was a cartoon under the heading "Strange but True, Little Known Facts for Catholics," distributed by the news service of the National Catholic Welfare Conference (the American hierarchy) during the summer of 1965. Drawn by M. J. Murray, it portrayed a wolf's head with this inscription beneath:

" 'Five pounds in cash for the head of a wolf or of an Irish priest.' This was the incredible and cruel reward by the government of Oliver Cromwell during penal days in Ireland in the seventeenth century."

The theological disagreements between Catholics and Protestants in Europe during the first decades of the schism were decided often on battlefields and on chopping blocks. In an America where the English colonists found themselves flanked on either side by the priests and trappers of Catholic powers, it was logical that an imported anti-Catholic bias would flourish, and it did. Monsignor Ellis reminds us that "a universal anti-Catholic bias was brought to Jamestown in 1607 and vigilantly cultivated in all the thirteen colonies from Massachusetts to Georgia." Virginia passed a law against Catholics in 1642. Massachusetts did the same five years later. The English revolution of 1688 saw the Church of England established by law in Maryland and New York; the then century-old penal law against Catholics of England and Ireland was fastened on the Catholics of New York and Maryland. By 1790 only five of the thirteen states allowed equal citizenship to Catholics.

In 1785, as Monsignor Ellis records, there were a mere 25,000 Catholics in an America of 4 million inhabitants. The marvel is less that this should have left a traumatic memory in American Catholic minds, but rather that the Catholic faith should have survived.

The help of Catholic France during the Revolution was a turning point. George Washington's attitude was appreciative. Laws against Catholics holding office relaxed. But then five immense historic influences were brought to bear on the frail plant of American Catholicism. There were:

1. An incredible wave of immigration which flowed until the start of the third decade of this century.

2. An almost complete ascendancy of the Irish inside the bishoprics of the country.
3. A sorry struggle between laymen and bishops over the issue of "trusteeism."
4. A papal repudiation of the heresy of "Americanism."
5. A condemnation by St. Pope Pius X of "modernism."

Each of these is still part of the bone structure of American Catholicism.

The extent of the immigration into the former English colonies from heavily Catholic areas of even Ireland, Germany and, later, of Italy and Poland is indicated by research done by Gerald Shaughnessy and reported in his book, *Has the Immigrant Kept the Faith?*[2] The beleaguered post-Revolutionary Catholic community of 25,000 received reinforcements of forty times its size between 1790 and 1850—1,071,000 Catholic immigrants in all. In the following half century the increase was sevenfold, half of it by immigration. The Catholic population rose to 12,041,000 in 1900. The essential strides had been taken toward the four times larger American Catholic Church of today, a mammoth of 50 million, producing half the world's Catholic religious vocations.[3] For the rest of the Catholic world the American Church statistics of the middle nineteen sixties were a cause of awe: 58,652 priests, 179,954 nuns, 12,271 members of orders of brothers, well over 4,000 foreign missionaries.

Immigration and the natural increase inside a Catholic community concerned about the moral implications of birth limitations have helped make the cross-topped Catholic church a landmark everywhere, but American Catholic presence in civic life has been far inferior to the numbers. Is the traditional vast Irish influence on the clergy, in the hierarchy and inside the laity itself, one of the causes of this inadequacy? Certainly the determined way in which American Catholics have clung to their spiritual inheritance owes much to the Irish, but there is little doubt but that a good share of the ghettoism afflicting the Catholic contribution to the American society traces also to the Emerald Isle.

Catholic and Irish are so nearly synonymous in much of America that this reporter was mildly surprised in hyper-Catholic Rome to observe that the "Mcs" in the Rome telephone book took up only two inches of listings. In addition to my own name there were only nine others beginning with the typically Irish "Mc," meaning "son of." In a vague way I had expected pages of Mcs in the phone book of the captial city of the Church.

Another unexpected find was that the College of Cardinals, the body which elects popes, had only one Irish cardinal in the fifties, unless you added in Irish-American, Irish-Canadian, and Irish-Australian princes of the church. Then you got above half a dozen, but still less than a tenth.

In my own little parochial school the main influence had been a Dominican nun, Sister Candida, who had drilled us at the age of ten in the use of at least some accepted version of English instead of the elided Brooklynese which was our street tongue. The name of our school was "St. Patrick's," and it was years afterward before I learned that Sister Candida was "as Irish as Paddy's pig," a native of the Ould Sod. At her feet all of us learned that the Irish were the world's best people and that we ought to be tactfully and condescendingly tolerant to non-Irish. St. Patrick's, Brooklyn, in the middle twenties was an Irish enclave a few hundred yards in from the Atlantic Ocean. We were all being raised as Americans, as Catholics and as Irishmen, and none of us—pupils and teachers alike—seemed to know where one began and the other left off, or whether all three had been fused by nature itself.

The Irishism of much that was American Catholic even in the middle sixties was indicated by a Sunday Mass address by a curate in a North Shore, Long Island, New York church in the late winter of 1965–66.

"You will know by my accent," the assistant said with the contentment of one who had not lost his native brogue, "that I hope all of you will come and enjoy our St. Patrick's Day dance."

There was a day when a vast share of America's bishops and a great many of her priests were Irish-born. The priest's speech made clear that the inflow of clergy from Ireland still had not ceased as the final third of the 1900s began.

And then there was the note which Father Patrick G. Branigan sent on the letterhead of the Holy Name Society of St. Peter Alcantara Church, Port Washington, Long Island, in late 1965:

"Dear parishioner: Every year, around St. Patrick's Day, the Holy Name Society . . . holds its annual dance. . . . Sometimes, even, we manage to persuade our Bocinos and Scarafamonis and Majinskis to become Irish for a few hours. . . . The entertainment committee informs me that the tickets will be ten dollars per couple, and to each table of ten persons there will be given two bottles of liquor, either Scotch or Rye. The music for the evening will be supplied by a New York society band. . . . So, for St. Patrick's sake! . . . Yours in Christ. . . ."

The Irish impact on the American Catholic Church during the middle years of the nineteenth century could be seen reflected in the 1850 census. By that date there were 961,719 Irish in the country, the greater share of them Catholic and most of them (like the writer's paternal grandparents) from famine-ravaged South Ireland. The sum was thirty-eight times the total American Catholic population of the immediate post-Revolutionary period. By the time of the second plenary council of the American hierarchy in October, 1866, eleven of the forty-five bishops who attended were natives of Ireland. Only fourteen had been born in the United States. The French, who had played a major role in the first decades of the United States Catholic Church, were by then second to the Irish. Ten of those at the council were French natives.

Three each were sons of Canada and Spain, and one each had been born in Austria, Belgium, Germany and Switzerland.[4]

By then, we know, there were some who were dubious about the concentrated Irish influence. Monsignor Ellis in *American Catholicism* tells of the letter the French-trained English-born Archbishop James Whitfield of Baltimore sent in 1832 to Bishop Joseph Rosati of St. Louis when a search was on for a successor to the late Bishop Edward Fenwick of Cincinnati: "If possibly a good choice can be made, let an American-born be recommended and (between us in strict confidence) I do really think we should guard against having more Irish bishops."[5]

So far as it affected Irish-American representation among the cardinals, archbishops and bishops of the next century, the Baltimore archbishop might have saved himself the bother, but an appropriate question is why the Maryland prelate felt as he did. To that, too, Monsignor Ellis suggests an answer in a quotation from Edmund Burke's letter on the penal laws against Catholics in Ireland: "It was a machine . . . as well fitted for the oppression, impoverishment, and degradation of a people, and the debasement in them of human nature itself, as ever proceeded from the perverted ingenuity of man."[6]

The Ireland I saw reflected in Sister Candida's classes in the middle twenties in St. Patrick's parochial school had been cut off from higher education and denied a free exercise of the Catholic religion of its people. It was largely separated from books and driven back into a hostile, closed-off attitude. It seemed often to me that it was not so much Roman Catholic in an affirmative way as in opposition to the anti-Romanism of England, a sort of double protestantism, a protest against the English protest. Such a mentality condemned much and supported little. It saw flaws but felt little responsibility. What America was like for the ragged hordes of Catholic Irish arriving in the middle of the nineteenth century is suggested by a plaque long displayed on the walls of New York's old St. Patrick's Cathedral. The sign told how men of the parish had taken up arms to defend the Church against the anti-Catholic nativist Know-Nothing movement. How logical that the arriving Catholic clergy should have seen parallels to the plight in their homeland and should have fostered their original mentality in the new land.

As a reporter in New York before World War II, I had occasions to see the lingering depths of the detached Irish, anti-English, feeling at rallies at which anti-Semites and pro-Nazis defended Hitler and argued against America becoming involved in Europe's "internal wars." An old ethics professor of my Catholic college (Fordham) introduced me privately to a German representative. Over beer in a bar he urged my support for Hitler's annexation of Austria.

"We Germans," he said soothingly, "are too harsh, it's true. The soft qualities of the Austrians will mellow and improve us."

He was a professional Hitler propaganda agent. I finished the beer and our acquaintanceship.

This same anger against England and willingness to sit out any constructive role inside the civic life of America was observed by Dr. Charles Fenwick, a Bryn Mawr professor, who stumped Catholic meetings after World War I in a fruitless effort to win support for President Wilson and the League of Nations.[7] He contended that St. Thomas Aquinas, Leo XIII and Benedict XV in his 1920 encyclical letter, "Pacem Dei" (God's peace), had argued for a close-knit family of nations; but in all his speeches to the predominantly Irish and German Catholics, Dr. Fenwick remembered later, "I never won a single debate or converted a single audience." The Irish wanted to hear only about Irish independence; the Germans were offended by the stern Versailles peace terms.

One meeting stood out in the memory of the propagandist for the League. A handsome and imposing Irish priest rose at the end, thanked the visitor politely, and then set everything in what he considered the right perspective:

"Doctor, we can't understand why you've not said a word about our dear Ireland. We demand to know why your League of Nations ignores that green, shimmering jewel in the Irish Sea, that lovely land for which so many fine men have suffered, died and been jailed. We want to know why your proud, imperious President Wilson even refused to see the fine men in the Irish delegation who asked him for just a few minutes. Why, doctor, was Ireland ignored while freedom was given to lands we've never heard about and can't even pronounce, places like Montenegro and Czechoslovakia?"

The opening assault on the League, its successful demolition so far as the immensely important American participation was concerned, was made before a largely Irish and German audience at a *Chicago Tribune* rally, Dr. Fenwick recalled.

Irish and Catholic were two words to express the same meaning in much of the America of the mid-twentieth century, but it is essential to an understanding of the new Catholic Church in the United States to note that a deep transformation was at work by the middle sixties both in Ireland itself and in the Church of the United States.

The new Ireland was reflected on May 1, 1965, in *America,* a Jesuit weekly with a largely Irish-American staff. *America* remarked that a visiting Irish priest had headed home after a United States tour with the comment that "I am going back to the nineteenth century." The Jesuits said in an editorial:

Perhaps he was. But Ireland is moving into the twentieth century fast—faster than many of her churchmen realize, and at a pace they are not prepared to cope with.

It is not impossible to conjure up a vision of a new Ireland:

42

more industrialized, therefore more urbanized, more in touch with the rest of the world, more modern—and pagan.

It troubles some intelligent Irish Catholics: it ought to trouble them all.

Not that there is the slightest use in trying to stem Irish economic progress or in denouncing modernity and all its works. A new Ireland is being born and welcome to it. We only want to say that it needs an alert and resourceful Irish Catholicism.

A glance through the *Annuario Pontificio* (the Pontifical or Vatican Yearbook) in the early 1960s showed 60 percent of the American Catholic bishops with Irish-sounding names (O'Brien, O'Flanagan, Gilmore, Maguire, O'Hara, Hogan, McEntegart) , but importantly there were two-fifths reflecting other national heritages: Morkowsky, Zuroweste, Bohachevsky, Grutka, Schexnayder, Pernicone.

The Irish-Americans themselves were in full evolution. In doing research for this book the harshest comments about the Irish role in American Catholicism were drawn from an editor and publisher with an Irish name, Edward M. Keating, of the vaguely Catholic, iconoclastic, minority-shielding *Ramparts* of California. He wrote to me:

Probably the most disastrous aspect to Catholicism in this country resides in the presence of the overwhelming dominance of the Irish clergy. This sort of thing has resulted in this country in an almost fatal disease of clericalism, the only antidote being anti-clericalism. This is not to say that I am anti-clerical since I have a whole host of clerical friends, but it is the institution of clericalism that is hounding people out of the Church and stupefying, if not terrifying, those who remain in the Church.

Perhaps characteristic Irish pessimism deepened the bitterness of the self-examination which Irish-American intellectuals, Catholics and apostates alike, conducted in the middle sixties, but three points were evident:

The Irish and the embattled Middle Western German Catholic clergy of the late 1800s and early 1900s made many

43

positive contributions, for the defensive walls they erected around the immigrant gave him some love, some status and some protection when a hospital, an orphan asylum or even a system of insurance was needed. Further, they made it possible for the Catholic spiritual and moral tradition to grow as an added value on American soil.

A new generation of Irish-American liberals in the hierarchy, clergy and laity were changing the nature of the Irish contribution.

The non-Irish at last were reaching pinnacles of power inside American Catholicism, bringing their varied inspirations as a reinforcement to earlier Irish accomplishments. This was emphasized in one of the little noted deeds of Pope John XXIII. When John ascended the papal throne in 1958, this was the background of the twelve cardinals of American Catholic history:

Irish-born, two: John Murphy Farley, of New York, and John Glennon, of St. Louis, whose elevation to Catholicism's governing body this writer witnessed in 1946, nearly at the half-century mark of the 1900s.

Son of two Irish-born parents, two: John McCloskey, of New York, and Dennis Dougherty, of Philadelphia.

Son of one Irish-born parent, two: Samuel Stritch, of Chicago, another whose promotion to the cardinals' college this reporter watched in 1946, and J. Francis A. McIntyre, of Los Angeles, who was appointed as late as 1953.

Descendant of wholly Irish stock, four more: William O'Connell, of Boston, Patrick J. Hayes, of New York, Edward Mooney, of Detroit, and Francis J. Spellman, of New York. The latter was the prelate who wielded the most potent single influence inside American Catholicism during the middle third of this century.

Not of Irish background, one: New York-born George Mundelein, of Chicago, whose parents were German by descent.

Pope John added two more Irish-Americans to the College of Cardinals in 1958—Richard James Cushing, of Boston, son of two parents born in Ireland, and John O'Hara, of Philadelphia, son of an American diplomat of Irish descent. Then in 1959 and 1961 John appointed three times as many non-Irish cardinals as the American Church had had in all of its history: the Milwaukee-born Aloisius Muench, Albert Gregory Meyer of Chicago, and Joseph Ritter of St. Louis, all of them of German origin. I chatted occasionally in Rome with Cardinal Muench, a Vatican diplomat, during his terminal illness in the early sixties. Cardinal Meyer, too, lived only for a few more years, but during the first part of the 1960s the German-Americans Meyer and Ritter established themselves as the liberal intellectual leaders of the American hierarchy at the critically important ecumenical council. One of the other three United States cardinals played a somewhat progressive council role, Richard Cushing. The remaining two, Cardinals Spellman and McIntyre, were in the conservative minority.

Irish names, especially in the older generation, popped up frequently in any review of American Catholic conservatism. In the 1930s it was Father Charles Coughlin. In the 1950s it was the layman Senator Joseph McCarthy, whose name became a synonym for scant concern about individual liberties. In the 1960s Yale-educated William F. Buckley, Jr., a deft debater, punctured the intellectual balloons of fuzzy-minded liberals, exposing some blunders and throwing roadblocks in the path of racial reforms and other social advances. "Sitting Bull" was the nickname various of the clergy had for an especially intransigent East Coast prelate of Irish origin. The one priest taken onto the national governing body of the rightist John Birch Society was a son of two Irish-born parents, Father John Fenton, pastor of the Blessed Sacrament Church of Bridgeport, Connecticut.

Conversely, those of Irish descent led, too, in the promotion of the liberal ideas of Leo XIII, Pius XI, Pius XII, John XXIII and Paul VI, and in a reevaluation of Catholicism's place in this country. The priest known as "Monsignor New Dealer," John A. Ryan, a son of a bricklayer, composed a good part of the labor-oriented 1919 statement of the American hierarchy (minimum wages, child labor limitations). He lived to see all but a handful of his twenty-three proposals converted into United States law (largely during the Franklin D. Roosevelt period). Father John Courtney Murray, architect of the official new Catholic doctrine of religious freedoms; Martin Haverty Work, the tireless creator of an effective new progressive national organization of Catholic men (son of two Irish-born parents); James O'Gara of *Commonweal;* the White House Kennedys; the Pat Crowleys (a husband and wife team leading the Christian Family Movement, the largest, most imaginative and most effective American Catholic group of the post-World War II period); the late Philip Murray, head of the Congress of Industrial Organizations; Cardinal Gibbons, a foresighted opponent of a separate American Catholic labor movement; Daniel Callahan, author of *The Mind of the Catholic Layman;* Phyllis McGinley; Bob Considine; Father Vincent O'Keefe, world director of Jesuit educational activities in the late sixties; Father Leo McLaughlin, author of a daring educational speed-up plan as president of Fordham University; Archbishop Joseph T. McGucken, of San Francisco, a campaigner for Negro rights—backward and forward through American Catholic history Irish names appeared over and over again in the list of those widening horizons and speeding an evolution which had begun aboard famine ships outside Irish ports over a century earlier.

The Irish and immigrant quality which hindered much lay initiative and activity in the middle 1800s was accompanied by another incident of American Catholic history which continued to stunt the United States Catholic social and civic contribution at the beginning of this century's final third. That was the trusteeship quarrel of the early 1800s. It is doubtful that as much as one percent of United States Catholics ever have heard of it, but in that one percent could be counted all 275 members of the hierarchy. Many of the bishops were still fearful that a vigorous lay moral, philosophical and social apostolate might fan trusteeship coals back into flames again.

This is not to suggest that the bishops of the country did not want the help of some sort of Catholic Action, but there was little doubt that none wanted a revival of a trusteeship battle which threatened the heart of the Catholic ecclesiastical organization just over a century ago.

"Trusteeism" was a pallid offense compared with those of the pope-naming Marozias and Crescenti of Rome's tenth century, but it shook the American Catholic structure nonetheless. It contributed to a deeper silencing of the mute man in the pew. In the middle 1960s Monsignor Vincent A. Yzermans, the engagingly, and wisely frank spokesman of the American hierarchy in Washington, conceded that the distant recollection of trusteeism continued to form many episcopal attitudes. The National Council of Catholic Men, the official organization of the male laity of the country, conceded in a "youth leadership" training course in 1963 that the "memory [of trusteeism] lingered in the minds of our churchmen and made them understandably wary of the lay apostolate."

Trusteeism grew up under the first American Catholic archbishop, John Carroll, of Baltimore. Laymen ran the temporal affairs of the parishes. This served as an antidote to nativist Protestant complaints that Catholicism was undemocratic, that bishops could appoint and dismiss pastors as they chose.[8] At the eve of the American Civil War, the system was still more useful. Know-Nothing legislation had forbidden clergymen in New York State to own property in their own name.[9]

But the coin was double-sided. Power bred an American

lay taste for more authority, and laymen tried to control the appointment of pastors, especially in parishes where an ethnic group wanted a shepherd of its own nationality. In a mixed Irish, German, French population the nationalism was dangerously divisive, and the challenge to episcopal authority was plain. Although Monsignor Ellis recalls that there were parishes in New Orleans, Charleston, Norfolk and Buffalo which were in schism for years, the bishops fought the lay trustees for control, and finally in the mid-1800s won. The importance of this historical episode in creating the all-powerful bishop and the docile layman of the mid-twentieth century was recognized by Boston's Cardinal Cushing in a pastoral letter on Good Shepherd Sunday of 1963, urging his laity to shoulder again their share of the Church apostolate. He wrote:

> It was in part by Archbishop Carroll's wish that in many places even the corporate ownership of Church property was placed in the hands of lay trustees. Unstable conditions within the Church eventually required that this experiment be abandoned, but the tensions arising out of it brought on a distrust of lay participation that has lingered in some part even to our own day.

In the cardinal's view, however, the problem of absorbing the hundreds of thousands of poor and often unlettered immigrants was an even more important factor in creating what amounted to a clerical monopoly of initiative. He said:

> Even more than this [trusteeship] failure . . . the rapid growth of the Church through immigration forced upon the clergy the burdens of policy and administration. Most of the laity, refugees from oppression and poverty in many lands, were not prepared by either education or experience to take an active part in the work of the Church. . . . Among the laity the emphasis was placed on strengthening loyalty to the faith and to the institutional Church.

The free, democratic, self-reliant air of America had its influence on the young American Catholic Church in the final years of the nineteenth century when laymen, working with the bishops, organized a thoughtful discussion of the American Catholic experience in Baltimore in 1889.[10] The self-appraisal was realistic, and relations with non-Catholics were treated with a broad spirit. But two inhibiting events followed quickly on the heels of one another: papal condemnations of the heresy of "Americanism" and of "modernism." Church scholars labored hard to prove that what French conservatives considered "Americanism" had never been a significant factor in the United States. In like fashion there was pious acceptance of St. Pius X's strictures against modern distortions of essential elements of the faith. The clergy, as the teachers of the Church, took over the task of steering the ship of religion through the surging doctrinal waters. The emergence of a broad and active American Catholic lay apostolate was put off to another day.

THREE

Ghetto Catholic

A long chat one afternoon in early 1966 in a motel room in midtown Manhattan summed up for this writer the startling change which came to the American lay Catholic as the final third of the twentieth century began. The man with whom I talked was not a layman and not even a native of the United States. Until a few months before, he had been a professor in a Baltimore seminary. He was Belgian-born Father Gommar De Pauw, the head of the Catholic Traditionalist Movement.

The "Catholic Traditionalists" were a small group of laymen, flanked no doubt by some old clergy who sympathized silently with Father De Pauw. They deplored the change from an all-Latin Mass to one which was almost wholly in English. They were shocked by the way in which the American bishops, the ecumenical council and the pope had swept away so much of familiar parish devotional exercises. They were distressed by indications that almost all inherited patterns, even in doctrine, seemed to be rejected as "nonessentials" of Catholicism and Christianity, and even as errors. They fought to turn back the clock. And Father De Pauw, a priest who wanted only to see things stay as they were, discovered himself under an ecclesiastical ban, stripped of his priestly rights.

"We don't ask that there be no Mass in English," the amiable middle-aged priest explained earnestly but with a smile, "We insist merely that there be a Mass each day in Latin for those who wish it. And we do protest against impieties of which we have heard. I was told about one priest who burst a rosary in the pulpit, scattering the beads on the floor. 'No more of this,' he said."

Devotion to the old Latin Mass, affection for the rosary, loyalty to the old ways, these were the priest's guidelines. But having taken his stand the Baltimore professor had found the evolving Church moving on without him. The ecumenical council had weighed more than sentimental attachment to the status quo, more than an aging man's fond memories of the customs of his youth. It had recognized that four centuries of rigidity, four hundred years of defending a multitude of medieval ways against Protestantism and the modern world, had created gross anachronisms in the convents, in the seminaries, in the parishes, in the popular devotions of the laity, in the lay role in the Church itself. The council used its sovereign powers to promulgate adaptation, evolution; a single priest in Baltimore, followed at least from afar by thousands of bewildered American laity, tried to say the council and the American hierarchy nay. The priest's situation was pathetic.

"It was not easy to cut myself off from what I had at the seminary," Father De Pauw said. "I was comfortably provided for there. For a half year now I have had no regular income as a priest, although some persons have sent me help."

The cardinal of Baltimore, Lawrence Shehan, a leader in official American Catholic efforts to seek a more brotherly relationship with Protestants as fellow Christians, saw the arguments for change. He descried no error, no betrayal, in forming new ways adapted to the life of literate, plural America. To him the professor's resistance was a scandal. He forbade Father De Pauw to say Mass, and denied that the process of transferring the priest to another diocese (Tivoli in Italy) had been completed.

"But it was," the professor insisted to me, "the Tivoli bishop expected approval from Cardinal Shehan and gave me documents as one of his priests. It's no concern of mine now whether Cardinal Shehan says that he started to comply and then changed his mind. And it doesn't matter if the bishop of Tivoli says he was hasty. I have the papers making me a Tivoli priest and that's all that concerns me. What the cardinal of Baltimore says [forbidding him to act as a priest] has nothing to do with me. I say Mass every day but each morning in a different parish. I show the pastor my Tivoli papers and he has no choice but to let me use an altar. But I shift each day because I don't want newspaper photographers to follow me.

"If Cardinal Shehan disagrees with me let him take it to the Rota [the Vatican court]. I don't care what the Apostolic Delegate [the papal representative in Washington] says about it. He speaks for the Secretariate of State [the pope's "prime ministry"] and that has nothing to do with matters of this sort. It's for the Rota to determine this. And even if the Rota acted against me I wouldn't submit. I'd appeal to the pope. And if he decided against me? Well, I just don't know what I would do then."

To some Catholics the priest's actions were shockingly disobedient and irreverent, even sacrilegious. To other thousands of the laity who used John Birch Society arch-right-wing bookstores to get tickets to the priest's lectures, Father De Pauw was a martyr to an effort to save a devotional way of life which could not be altered or abandoned without shaking the foundations of faith itself.[1] To me Father De Pauw was a well-intentioned but misguided churchman who understood neither the need for vast, permanent adaptations in an enduring global faith, nor the extent of the demands for obedience and submission which organization and unity impose.

"How's your Latin?" I asked Father De Pauw as I took leave.

"Good if I must say so," he grinned with the pleasure of a student who had managed to convert the dead language of Rome to one of current conversational value. "I insisted on teaching theology to my seminarians in Baltimore in Latin for ten minutes out of every hour, but I couldn't demand more than that. I had to do the rest in English. These Americans, they just don't know Latin."

The smile of the justly proud man of culture curved the corners of the churchman's lips.

Father De Pauw stood alone as the sole priest of nearly 60,000 in the United States to react so strongly, openly and defiantly, but there is no doubt that he symbolized shock suffered by many of the tens of millions of American Catholic faithful. As Father Robert J. Welch, of the School of Religion of the State University of Iowa, said at the 27th Annual Michigan Pastors Conference at the University of Michigan in Ann Arbor at the start of 1966, "Many Catholics took everything as a package deal, as straight out of Revelation." How could any part of the old acts of reverence be subtracted without placing all belief in question?[2]

The extent of the distress felt by Catholics in the wake of Vatican Council II can best be measured by considering how far from modern American life various pious practices and attitudes of the laity had drifted as a result of four hundred years of Counter-Reformation and a century of parochially withdrawn life on American soil. A scanning of the pages of the magazines and newspapers sold on parish book racks provided endless, astonishing examples of the strange devotional world of their own into which various of the laity tended to slip. Clergy sometimes provided the leadership in this, and businessmen were eager accomplices. Following are examples.

Drugs, foods, alcohol, articles and institutions of all kinds sold or promoted under a religious label

The Tablet, the highly conservative weekly paper of the traditionalist Brooklyn diocese, carried an ad for a loaf of bread on April 2, 1964. It illustrated the point. The heart of the advertisement was a sketch of a friar, his cowled head bent in contemplation. "Monk's Bread," said the headline. The copywriter took it from there:

This bread may very well make the best toast you ever tasted. Monk's Bread has a flavor you can't toast away. Even butter can't hide it. It has a goodness you don't find in most bread. It's a bread that wasn't meant to be sold. It began as a simple sustenance for the monks at the Abbey of the Genesee—men who eat no meat, no fowl. All the good things the monks baked into their full-flavored loaf naturally toast up better. Try Monk's Bread tomorrow, toasted. The . . . Baking Company bakes Monk's Bread for you using the exact pre-packaged formula delivered to the bakery, special Monk's Bread pans, and following a strict preparation schedule under guidance of the abbey.

One could confidently hope that the Abbey of the Genesee received a donation from the baker, but the attempt to sell monks' "goodness" toasted would have turned any but a ghettoist stomach.

Father Thomas E. Clarke, a Jesuit, was sensitive to commercialization of this sort as he pointed out in the May 29, 1965, issue of *America.* Like many another stroller on Rome's Via del Corso (the Broadway of ancient Rome) he had been startled to come across the Banco di Santo Spirito, the "Holy Ghost's bank." Where could a pious Italian investor place his funds with greater confidence than in the very stronghold of the Trinity's Third Person? Father Clarke wrote:

. . . religious names on the Banco di Santo Spirito, and breads and wines, and hotels and aspirins and cough medicines. . . . And then, what of hospitals and welfare organizations? More delicately still, what of institutions of learning? Should we not also say that a poem is a poem is a poem, or an atom is an atom is an atom, and leave the non-religious aspects of education and scholarship unembarrassed by religious preoccupations . . . ? [Father] Karl Rahner . . . is in the forefront of those calling upon the Church to recognize that her medieval stance toward the world is no longer possible."

"Cute" sideline items of religion

The catalogue of the Abbey Press (St. Meinrad, Illinois) ran this item reprinted by Dan Herr, conductor of the witty "Stop Pushing!" column of *The Critic,* a publication dedicated to intellectual Catholicism: " (Children's costumes). The little cardinal. Red cassock with attached shoulder cape, red and gold sash, red biretta, white collar, crucifix, $8.95 net. . . ."

If readers of Mr. Herr's column thought he might have invented part of the item, they needed only to examine the ad run on October 21, 1965, in *The Long Island Catholic.* Hallowe'en, it pointed out, is not just an evening of tomfoolery for tots who dress up outlandishly and beg candy door to door. It is the Catholic feast of All Hallows' Eve, the day before All Saints' Day. The ad was signed by two men with appropriately "holy" Irish names. To "celebrate the *religious* meaning of the occasion," it invited customers to spend $3.50 for any of twenty-three "religious Hallowe'en costumes." Among those offered were:

St. Joseph
Priest (vested or in cassock)
Cardinal
Bishop
Pope

GHETTO CATHOLIC

St. Michael, the archangel
Knight crusader
The Blessed Mother
Saint (girl or boy)
Nun (black, brown, white, blue, grey or novice)
Bride
Angel
Martyr

All costumes were guaranteed to be 100 percent cotton broadcloth, size 6. Charge for sizes 10 to 12, $3.95.

"Cry Pax," another satirical column, this one in *The Catholic Reporter* of Kansas City, found the following advertisement and reported it on January 14, 1966. It ran in the name of a New Jersey manufacturer who had helped build the simple throne chair which Pope Paul VI used during an evening Mass in the New York Yankee Stadium baseball park on October 4, 1965, during history's first visit of a pope to the Western hemisphere. The throne had been a simple block-shaped affair. The chair-builder must have obtained some of the scrap lumber after the temporary altar structure was demolished for he offered five-inch models of the stadium throne done "by the same worker" who built the pontifical chair, and containing a plug of wood which had been "encased in the altar blessed by Paul VI" at the ball park. The altar, the manufacturer pointed out, had been "used at the [pope's] Mass for peace." Charge for the tiny wood reconstruction: $17.95.

The rosary in many forms

The simple rosary, a prayer to Christ's Mother which even an illiterate can learn with no difficulty (the Hail Mary repeated fifty-three times, the Lord's Prayer said six times, and the Apostles' Creed recited once) seemed to attract special imaginative efforts, possibly because it was a distinctive devotion separating Catholics from most other Christians. One manufacturer offered a transparent rosary with a statue inside each bead. *Columbia* magazine, the publication of the Knights of Columbus, carried ads for "kiddie rosaries" ($1.95, the beads multicolored and nontoxic). For adults there were "aurora borealis" rosaries (clear crystal, wine or milk white, $12.95). Monumental rosaries were conceived too. Dan Herr reported in the December 6, 1965, *The Critic* that he had come across this in the July-August, 1965, *Our Lady's Digest:* "The Benedictine Sisters of Holy Family Convent, Benet Lake, Wisc., have an outdoor rosary made up of bowling balls. One hundred and fifty rose bushes connect the beads."

Finally, there was the world's largest rosary at Our Lady of Fatima Shrine, Holliston, Massachusetts. It weighed 350 tons. Each bead was a five-foot cube of granite, bearing a copper plate on which the Hail Mary was written in fifty-three languages. The white marble crucifix was life-sized. It took a walk of just under a fifth of a mile to "do" that rosary. It was designed "to enable families to pray together."

Fringe ideas playing at the edges of the pious instinct are as many as the human imaginations which have applied themselves to man's problems and to the possibilities of commerce. *Alert Catholic Men,* a bulletin of one-paragraph feature items, inspirational and entertaining (distributed by the National Council of Catholic Men to affiliated organizations), carried this pedicure comment in February, 1965: "Have you got bunions? Go barefoot and forget them. Medical doctors, foot specialists, say no bunions on Poor Clare nuns because they wear sandals in winter and go barefoot in summer."

Even a father of Vatican Council II, Bishop Fulton J. Sheen, famous as the American television priest, cooperated with one medal promotion idea. In his nationally syndicated column as head of the American Catholic Society for the

Propagation of the Faith, an official Church subsidiary, he ran this in January, 1966:

The God Love You medal, a lovely Madonna of the World, is one you would be proud to give and delighted to receive. Designed by the world-renowned jeweler, Harry Winston, and blessed by Bishop Sheen, it is available in a classic Florentine gilt finish or sterling silver. Send your request and corresponding offering to The Society for the Propagation of the Faith, 366 Fifth Avenue, N.Y., N.Y. 10001. $2 small silver; $3 small 10K gold-filled. Cut out this column. Pin your sacrifice to it. . . .

During the same period *The Catholic Cook Book* was offered for sale in an ad in *The New York Times. The Catholic Reporter* of January 7, 1966, noted that the volume was extolled as "probably the second most important book for the Catholic home," outranked only by Scripture, and that there was even a recipe for "skewered beef Roman-style for the Feast of St. Anthony." *The Catholic Reporter* was distressed. It commented that "one liturgically addled source" had offered a topper: "vanilla pudding with cherry sauce for the Feast of the (massacre of the) Holy Innocents."

Even such an outgoing and modern paper as *The Long Island Catholic,* published for an instructed New York commuter readership, regularly carried a column in 1966 called "The Catholic Traveler." Diligent reading of the offering indicated that Catholics who journey seem to enjoy much the same museums, beaches and scenery as those which appeal to "non-Catholic tourists."

The separatist tendency by no means limited itself to advertising of commercial products and to concepts on religion's margins. The world upon which the modernizations of Pope John XXIII and Vatican Council II burst so suddenly had many devotional practices which had wandered far from the Mass and from the broad, world-encompassing concepts of Christianity's early years. Novenas of various types, the cult of saints traditionally seen as the apostles of certain qualities, and a narrow fervor raising the question of superstitious overtones were common in a part of American Catholic life of the early 1960s and were reflected in the pages of many small journals published by certain religious orders. A reporter remembers the words of Archbishop Francis J. Spellman as he arrived in New York just at the start of World War II to become spiritual leader of the Catholics of Manhattan and of adjoining counties. "I will pray," the future cardinal said, "as if everything depended on God, and I will work as if everything depended on me."

Reading the ads of various of the novenas and shrines, it was easy to doubt that the same modern spirit of industry and self-reliance went always hand in hand with the prayers of each client. The Jesuits' *Sacred Heart Messenger* of January, 1965, for instance, carried these "thanksgivings to the Sacred Heart," under a quotation from Ecclesiastes, XXXVI, 6, "Renew Thy signs and work Thy miracles":

 1 conversion
 1 amputation averted
 7 operations averted
26 successful operations
 2 successful dental work
 3 peace of mind
10 property sold
 9 safe journey
13 favorable diagnoses
 3 normal child
 6 successful examinations
 3 homes found
26 recoveries
 7 happy deaths

For those on Catholic mailing lists it was not uncommon to receive letters such as one sent out "prayerfully yours in St. Jude" from the Church of St. John the Baptist in Baltimore, identified as the national shrine of "St. Jude, the saint of the impossible."

One such letter came quickly to the point:

Dear friend,

St. Jude can help you. . . . Do you have a problem? Do you feel depressed? Are you on the verge of despair? If you feel this way, I (the undersigned priest) recommend that you turn to St. Jude in your hour of need. . . .

I'll never forget the reaction of the businessman who came. . . . To call St. Jude the saint of the impossible was to him a clever and catchy slogan—sort of a commercial—designed to impress the imagination and give people a crutch to lean on as they wrestle with the more serious problems. "Unbelievable" was all he could repeat as he came to realize that he was so wrong about St. Jude. . . .

The businessman, said the letter, "poured" (sic) over letters in the shrine files and was overwhelmed with what he saw. "Mail me your petitions today," the letter invited. Enclosed was a checklist with twenty-six suggested favors which could be sought from "the saint of the impossible." The letter added that "you may check as many intentions as you choose." On the tersely worded list were:

Holy Father
Prodigal son
Better position
Increase in wages
Russia
Return to faith
Employment
Good friends
Sale of property
Eyesight
Financial aid

The possibility of a reader's lingering uncertainty was not overlooked. The letter said:

If you have any doubts, please read the following. . . .

"St. Jude Oil Helped.

"I was one of the skeptics who was giving up hope in St. Jude. Now, words can't express my gratitude. I was hurt at work and my right leg was so bad that I couldn't sleep in bed, on couch or on floor. I began using St. Jude Oil which you sent me a long time ago. The fourth day after I was able to sleep on the floor. And before the end of the week, I was sleeping in bed. If I wasn't helped I would have had to go to the hospital for the removal of a disc.

"Mr. L. J. G., Erie, Pa."

Six similar letters followed.

Strangely, the most advanced techniques of American selling are used to foster various of the special pieties which seem far removed from the twentieth-century world or from the Church of *aggiornamento,* of updating, which the instinctively brilliant Pope John XXIII summoned into being. The Marianist Mission of Dayton, Ohio, for instance, used Catholic mailing lists to send Mass cards for life's various events. One was addressed to "someone in sorrow." Another was for a "happy occasion." One said merely "thinking of you." One, narrowly, was for "someone named Mary." One intended to wish a "happy vacation," and offered the hope that "St. Christopher and God [would] be with you on your vacation," and said: "Prayer before a journey. Into the land of peace and prosperity direct us, O almighty and merciful God: and may the Angel Raphael accompany us in the way, and may we return in peace, health and joy unto our own home. From the missal." Even for one bound on a vacation trip recommended in *The Long Island Catholic*'s "Catholic Traveler" column, receipt of the "happy vacation" Mass card presumably would induce appropriately sober second thoughts. Each card pledged a year of Masses and a weekly rosary and Communion by Marianist seminarians. The note accompanying the cards invited the receiver to send offerings only at the time of actual use of each of the greetings.

GHETTO CATHOLIC

The ghettoist mentality is comfortable neither to the ever more numerous educated Catholics nor to thoughtful clergy. Bishop John J. Boardman, Brooklyn diocesan director of the Society for the Propagation of the Faith, complained in his weekly column in *The Tablet* of the sort of tavern-haunting world-of-his-own type of person who thrives in such a climate.

"We've had people call at 2 or 3 o'clock in the morning," the bishop said, "to ask some foolish question about fasting or abstinence, or what time the first Mass is, with the very distinct sounds of a blaring radio or night club orchestra in the background.

"When the sleepy voice would answer them in somewhat of a remonstrating manner, they would say, 'I thought you sat up by the phone all night, father, answering calls. Isn't that what the man on duty does?' "

Ghettoism, a consequence of poor education and isolation —separation both from the modern world and from the central inspirations of the renewed postconciliar Church— took many forms. Katherine Burton, the sophisticated author of the "Woman to Woman" column in *The Sign* magazine of the Passionist Fathers of Union City, New Jersey, told indignantly in her April, 1965, article of the slowness of the growth of the ecumenical spirit in some parts of the American Catholic world, so far as the Young Men's Christian Association and the Salvation Army were concerned. She said:

[I think of] a letter written to me some time ago by a troubled mother who had been forbidden—that was the word—to let her son use the YMCA swimming pool. The neighborhood was poor and the only other place to play was in the streets.

And I was reminded of another woman who wrote recently that at the church she attends the priest stood at the altar and said it was a sin to donate to the Salvation Army. . . . I read that the Santa Fe Archdiocese has just removed restrictions on Catholic participation in the YMCA, saying that their programs are "Christian and commendable."

The strange contradictions are suggested by a quarter of a page restaurant advertisement run March 24, 1966, in *The Long Island Catholic*, offering recipients of the Sacrament of Matrimony "the wedding of your dreams, at a price you never dreamed possible; starting at $7.95 per person . . . smorgasbord . . . epicurean delights . . . unlimited liquors, Rye, Scotch, Bourbon, Gin, Vodka, Manhattans, Martinis, Orange Blossoms, Screwdrivers, Cuba Libres, Daiquiris, Whiskey Sours . . ."

It was an odd little world of its own, the American Catholic community of the middle 1800s to the middle 1900s, and one worth recording if only because a changing, better instructed, post-Vatican II Church community was sure to eliminate much of it. An NCWC story from Chicago, which apeared in *The Tablet* on February 10, 1966, recorded, for instance, that "Novena Notes," which once had a circulation of 50,000, would cease publication after 29 years of life because "it's the end of an era for novenas," and the young are "much less inclined to public prayers."

The modern-minded *The Sign* of the Passionists used a short review of Mary Perkins Ryan's *Through Death to Life* in March, 1966, to praise her for "piquing pseudo-Christians whose approach to suffering and death is summed up: " 'I don't care if it rains or freezes,/ Long as I got my plastic Jesus/ Glued to the dashboard of my car.' "

Protestant fellow workers on my newspaper had taunted me about the dashboard saints and crucifixes which were the badge of Catholic separatism in New York and a kind of hex symbol against trouble in the middle sixties: "You get one for every Protestant you run over."

The Fatima devotion, in the hands of some members of the pious Catholic "Blue Army," was shaped in the late fifties into something hardly short of Fatimania. Three shep-

63

herd children had reported, in the poverty-shaken Portugal of 1917, that they had on several occasions seen what appeared to be the Virgin on the bleak plateau of Fatima. Two of the three children died soon, but the third, Lucy, became a cloistered nun. The three said that the Virgin had called for prayer and penitence, had emphasized the need for converting Russia, and had warned of calamities which might lie in store for a feckless world. A generation later Lucy added a few more messages which she said Mary had given her. She put them in a letter for the pope or for other Church dignitaries. Extreme Fatima devotees in the laity and among some of the clergy, fascinated by the thought that Heaven was communicating so articulately and so pertinently with a Moscow-threatened world, spread the word that Lucy's letter "might" predict the world's end in 1960.

The Fatima story without question added a new center of religious devotion to Europe's map. Tourists and pilgrims flocked to the Portuguese village in numbers rivaling those going to Lourdes, the French scene of other reported apparitions of Mary of the nineteenth century. Convents and churches costing millions of dollars rose where the peasant children had knelt. In 1930, Church officials, long skeptical, at last described the tots' tale as "worthy" to be believed. Permission was given to build parish churches and to install stained glass windows honoring Christ's mother in a new way, as "Our Lady of Fatima." Officially, though, the story of the phenomenon remained classed as "a private revelation" which each Catholic was free to believe or not as he chose.

Pius XII, a man combining great diplomatic and scientific sophistication with the uncomplicated faith of a child, reported in his final years in the nineteen fifties that he had seen the sun spin in the sky over the Vatican gardens, the sole abnormality reported in 1917 in Portugal by any but the three children. The pope, it was clear, thought that this might be a heavenly sign that the Fatima cult was justified.

Beyond that, however, I personally sensed much embarrassment as I discussed with other dignitaries Sister Lucy's comments at the Vatican in the late fifties, especially in the days just before New Year's Eve, 1959.

"End of the world in 1960!" one Holy See official exclaimed. "Do you think we'd be preparing for an ecumenical council in 1962 if we thought that? When will that letter be opened? When will it be published? Maybe never. This church is not run by private revelations."

Urbane Cardinal Fernando Cento, papal nuncio in Portugal at the time of most discussion of Lucy's letter, told me that he went to see the nun in her cloister, watched her use a camera as the convent's official photographer, and then listened as she commented: "A lie is wrong even in the service of the good."

"Remember that," the nuncio agreed.

The reserved Church position, refusing to exclude the possibility that the mother of Christ had spoken to people of this century, but reluctant to publish Lucy's latter-day compositions, was in no way reflected by the Fatima extremists. A writer to Monsignor J. D. Conway's "Question Box" in *The Catholic Reporter* for October 29, 1965, complained that "they derive from the Fatima apparitions that . . . anti-Christ is in our midst, just what fashions are immoral, and so forth: if you stop them for a minute to say, 'Well, that's possible, but . . . ,' they look at you as if you were a heretic." Father Daniel S. Hamilton in *The Long Island Catholic,* June 4, 1964, was asked about reports attributed to two priests that the Virgin gave Pius XII her veil to prove the truth of the Fatima story, and that a thread from the shawl was being venerated, in the fifties, as a relic at some mission services in the New York area.

"If you are over seven years of age," Father Hamilton straightened out the inquirer, "you should know that [the veil and thread story] is pure nonsense."

Monsignor Conway's correspondent remarked that "as far as I can see, if the Church attached such importance to these apparitions she would read passages from them in church instead of the Gospels and epistles, and would encourage study of them instead of the papal encyclicals."

The monsignor, like almost every other responsible American Catholic editor, had had a long experience with the far-out Fatima cultists. His answer reflected the weariness of one worn with the type of battle which can develop within the walls of a cut-off group:

"You said it, brother, so let them jump on you, not me. But you can be sure that they will jump, viciously. It is safer to stir up a hornets' nest."

Part II

John's Revolution

FOUR

The New Nun

The Catholic layman who, on weekdays, taught university classes, ran large businesses or served in the Senate and even in the White House could not remain forever mute and inert on Sunday mornings inside a church of limited clerical dimensions. The faith of some would fade. Others, however few, would insist on an intellectual and active faith and religious commitment. In the rather extreme view of Edward M. Keating, the editor of *Ramparts,* the rebellious, reformist California publication, "the appalling fact is that two-thirds of the registered Roman Catholics are alienated from the Church, and for legitimate reasons: these are the Catholics I wish to reach and, further, I wish to reach non-Catholics."

Mr. Keating was answering my question about what he was attempting to do with his private, Catholic-inspired, but by no means Catholic-establishment, magazine.

A revolution was inevitable as education increased and as the once-immigrant layman felt himself more and more a welcome and needed part of the American community, but the change might have been slower if it were not for a sequence of parallel revolutions, in Bible study, in theology, among women who sought a more central and honored place within the Church, among nuns, inside seminaries and among the clergy and hierarchy members themselves. To understand the forces working on the Catholic layman of America it is well to review these other explosions around him.

This writer was in the vast, marble-alabaster-and-mosaic Church of St. Paul outside Rome's walls on the afternoon in January, 1959, when stoop-shouldered, gnarled old John XXIII set off many of Catholicism's revolutions with a simple announcement: he would summon an ecumenical council to review the state of the Church and to bring Catholicism up to date.

About five thousand of us were in the old basilica over the believed burial place of St. Paul, Christianity's great early missionary. The pope sat through the services and then walked into the medieval cloister next door without saying anything to us in the congregation. Other eminent Church dignitaries should get his sensational news first, the pope believed. Accordingly, with a handful of men around him, a dozen of them cardinals, old Pope John made his announcement. No one commented. Later a few told the pope that the idea was such a good one that they could not find ways to express themselves. It seemed to me at the time that the opposite was clearly true. A council reopens dormant questions. How and where it finishes, perhaps decades after the closing ceremony, is anyone's guess. For weeks after that statement, official Catholic publications such as the authoritative Jesuit *Civiltà Cattolica* (Catholic Civilization) dragged heels about discussing the papal decision. It seemed evident that some, guided by conservatives such as the Vatican Secretary of State, Cardinal Domenico Tardini, hoped that aged Pope John could be dissuaded and that the dramatic idea might be dropped. The pope was well aware of conservative opposition inside his close official family.

"I must move cautiously," John, in effect, told a mutual

70

friend, who related the conversation to me. "I cannot just dismiss these conservatives. If I were to do that I could arouse sympathy for them. I cannot forget that I will be here as pope only for a short time. I must be careful not to start a reaction which might well end up with an arch-conservative as my successor."

The conservatives feared that open discussions and new thought would bring on insurrectional ideas which could sweep away not only anachronisms but essentials of the Christian faith as well. John, an optimist and a brave man, felt rather that times change and that the ways of presenting and organizing an ancient religious presence in the world must alter too, however difficult the adaptations. The revolutions sweeping so much of the Catholic world are now testing the insights of the old pope's inspiration. The changes may best be observed inside the convents where 180,000 American women are consecrating their virginal lives to God.

"The nuns have moved furthest," comments Monsignor Yzermans, the spokesman for the American hierarchy in Washington. "But then," the jolly Midwest German-Irish priest adds, "they had furthest to come."

What is going on among America's nuns was suggested at the daily American press briefings during the ecumenical council in Rome. Priest experts assigned by the United States bishops answered the questions of newsmen about each day's developments at the council sessions under St. Peter's dome. Sprinkled among the reporters were note-taking nuns from the United States, sent by their orders to find out exactly what vast changes in the Church were taking place. It was clear that the transformations occurring inside the council would have repercussions in many American convents long before some parishes and laity suspected the shifting stands.

On lecture tours in the early sixties I found a ferment among the nuns everywhere. At Misericordia, the Catholic girls' college in Dallas, Pennsylvania, nuns said that the simplification of their habit and easing of their rules had provoked two reactions: "The middle-aged sisters are nervous, but the very young and the very old accept it wholeheartedly. The reason the old approve is that they have passed a whole lifetime obeying, so they submit now too!"

At St. Mary of the Woods College in Indiana, sisters told me that they had read Belgian Leo Cardinal Suenens' book on the modernization of the convents with enthusiasm. In Louisville, Kentucky, the librarian of a college and of a sisters' generalate pointed to the works of the new liberal theologians in prominent places on her shelves. She added this bit: "They're all reading the new theology here, but some want me even to throw out the old theological works! I've refused. I make the point that at least they ought to be available. They were the foundation from which everything has come." So in her library the pietistic, medieval theology remained—unread.

Younger sisters and, less excitedly, older ones clamored for changes, many of them recommended by Cardinal Suenens. In letters to such remarkable clearinghouses for ideas as "The Sisters' Forum" in Kansas City's outspoken *The Catholic Reporter,* and in conferences and books, sisters asked over and over for an end to rules which treated them as less than children. They asked for a reduction in vocal prayer, an increased opportunity to substitute individually selected spiritual reading adapted to the different cultural levels of the consecrated women, and a change in dress reaching in some cases even so far as the use of contemporary streetwear. More chances to leave the convent to improve as professional specialists were on some sisters' lists. Greater contact with the laity in social work or in parent-teacher groups was another urgent request.

The wave of change reached even into the cloisters, though only a few weak ripples arrived there. Father Thurston N. Davis, the talented editor of the Jesuits' *America,* had a chuckly note in his weekly column on November 30, 1963, about a call he received from one strictly cloistered convent when Lyndon B. Johnson was running against Barry Goldwater for president of the United States. The mother superior of that convent had permitted *America* into the convent as its one link with the secular world, so it was natural that she should ask a nun friend to inquire of *America* how the sisters should go about registering and voting. Father Davis called a woman friend who had been a government official in Washington and she visited the convent. They turned out to be "wonderful girls" who did not know the difference between the mildly internationalist Mr. Johnson, the chauvinist Senator Goldwater or Robert F. Kennedy, brother of the late Catholic president who was engaging at that time in what proved to be a successful race for United States senator from New York.

Father Davis smiled in print: "But out to vote they were going, not at all hampered by this particular distinction. (There really *are* more important matters, after all.) Moreover, although they always wear rope sandals (alpargatas) in the convent, Mother Superior decided that people didn't vote in sandals. So every nun got a pair af leather 'voting' shoes."

Father Davis, a leader in American Catholic modernization, touched the "cute" note in talking about the cloistered nuns, but "cuteness" was precisely the quality many intelligent nuns least wished to have attributed to their vocation. The sleigh-riding, baseball-playing sisters who were the delight of news photographers in quest of the incongruous were not the educated, useful daughters of God and sisters of mankind whom legions of brighter United States nuns aspired to be.

How far the American sister had to "come," to use Monsignor Yzermans' expression, was reflected in a quotation from "By Rule, by Custom, by Unwritten Law," by Sister

Mary Gilbert, carried in *Convent Life,* edited by Joan M. Lexau.[1] Sister told what might happen if "Mrs. X" invited nuns of five orders out for a drive.

> Sister A may go for the ride, but she can't get out of the car or eat an ice-cream cone on the way. Sister B may go for the ride and get out of the car, but refreshments are taboo. Sister C may go for the ride and have her ice cream, but all within the sanctuary of the car. Sister D may go for the ride, get out of the car, and eat the ice-cream cone. She may even name her own flavor if Mrs. X isn't a dictator. Sister E? She may come out to the car and wave goodbye to the others.

Tensions and frustrations among nuns, some of them magnified by the second-class status of women everywhere within the Church, combined with liberal attitudes among various of the popes, cardinals and archbishops of the mid-twentieth century to guarantee that a rapid evolution would take place in Catholicism's convents. Pius XII, who deserves wider recognition as a pioneer in Catholic reform, opened a way with an instruction in 1952 to superiors of nuns' orders to "make sure that nothing in your customs, your manner of life, or your ascetical practices raises a barrier to vocations."

That there were difficulties in attracting recruits to the sisterhood was no secret. Father Ernest Schoenmaeckers, the Jesuit who was assistant director of the Apostleship of Prayer in Holland (a nation with ten times the Catholic world average in missionaries and seventeen times its proportional share of missioner priests), reported in *The Month* in London in June, 1965, that the number of candidates for the secular priesthood had fallen since World War II to half of what the expanding Dutch Catholic population could have been expected to provide. He added that the number of women going into the convents was even less; they were entering at one-third the prewar rate.

This did not imply that there were few. In the United

States in the middle sixties there were 180,000 women in religious orders, and throughout the whole of the Catholic world there were one million. (The proportion of American girls in convents was almost double the world Catholic average.) What the numbers did mean was that thoughtful members of the hierarchy persistently were returning to the problem of the best use of these armies of dedicated women, and to their adequate adjustment to a changing planet.

Pope Paul VI broke the tradition of sixteen centuries of ecumenical councils by inviting nuns and other women to serve as auditors at Vatican Council II. The American nun he chose was Sister Mary Luke, superior general of the Sisters of Loretto at the Foot of the Cross, and chairman of the Conference of Major Religious Superiors of Women, a group embracing most of the main American orders of sisters. The choice of Sister Mary Luke, the former Ruth Marie Tobin, was, in a sense, a special gesture of accord with the modern world for, until she decided to be a nun, the aesthetic Miss Tobin had run a Denver ballet school.

Paul's purpose, as he said, was "that women may know how much the Church honors them in the dignity of their being and in their human and Christian mission."[2]

The vigorous hierarchy movers in the cause of nuns and of other women, at least so far as the public could see, were Cardinal Suenens of Brussels and Atlanta's genial ex-newsman archbishop, Paul J. Hallinan. They were forthright, far-reaching and articulate. But as Father Yves Congar, the French Dominican theologian, told Anna Brady of *The Long Island Catholic* (April 16, 1964, issue), "I know [that Cardinal Suenens' dramatic autumn 1963 proposal to the ecumenical council that women auditors be invited was made] at the suggestion of the Holy Father [Paul VI]."

Be that as it may, I recall the joshing which gentle Archbishop Hallinan took one evening in the fall of 1965 in the dim light of the medieval square in front of the ancient church of Santa Maria in Trastevere (Holy Mary in the Cross-the-Tiber area), as fellow priests and bishops of the United States warned that American Catholic feminists would inundate his small Georgian diocese.

Bishop Robert Emmet Tracy of Baton Rouge, Louisiana, summed up the half-teasing but approving reaction of the liberal clergy with a note in *America* magazine, October 30, 1965. He said that a written proposal on women's rights in the Church which Archbishop Hallinan had just submitted to the ecumenical council "included everything that any feminist could ask for: active participation in liturgical functions, full education in theology with a view to consultation, a voice in the shaping of the new apostolate of the laity, representation in force on all bodies that seriously affect, by their decisions, the status and interest of women, and so on." The archbishop, said Bishop Tracy, could well "expect to be the target of interest of grateful women everywhere, and a positive hero to the feminists." And, he added, with the practical view of a bishop who knows what it is to try to lure the dedicated, low-paid nuns to staff the schools and other good works of a diocese, "he should do right well in getting religious Sisters for his schools." More importantly, the Baton Rouge prelate went on, "he has alerted the Fathers [of the ecumenical council] to the fact that the Church, in the past, has not really taken much of a lead in the emancipation of women from obvious discrimination and injustice." Both nuns and laywomen, Bishop Tracy said, had commented that the Hallinan presentation was a "perfect" statement of their common aspirations inside a male-dominated Church community.

The gist of the Hallinan recommendation was that women be ordained for the tasks they perform, and that vastly wider Church horizons be opened to them. He asked that they be allowed to serve as deaconesses, preaching, baptizing and giving Holy Communion to the faithful, that they act as lectors and acolytes at Mass, and that they perform all other functions assigned to laymen and to those males who proceed no further than the deaconate on the road toward the priesthood.[3] In short, the Atlanta prelate told the council, "we must not continue to perpetuate the secondary place accorded to women in the Church of the twentieth century."

Not only nun and lay women feminists applauded Archbishop Hallinan on this. Joe Breig, a prolific contributor to the American Catholic press, wrote in Notre Dame University's *Ave Maria* on December 11, 1965: "Personally, I have never been able to think of anything in the essential nature of the sacrament of Holy Orders which ought to exclude women from receiving it."

Cardinal Suenens' view was expressed on the floor of the council where he called for the acceptance of women at least as auditors. It was further clarified in interviews such as one with Desmond Fisher, editor of London's *Catholic Herald,* and also in the cardinal's book, *The Nun in the World.*[4] The prelate's case was simple: women are half the people of the world. The one million in the Catholic sisterhoods are, in many cases, prisoners of outdated rules, wasting vast potential resources and making little real impact on their times. "If every nun in the world could influence only five people to spur them on to apostolic effort, the world would soon be converted." If sisters would take up active charitable works such as the care of the sick and the old, the rearing of the young, and programs of adult education, they could accomplish "ten thousand times" more good. The cardinal's volume urged that sisters receive an adequate professional training, that old regulations be altered to allow apostolic service to the laity, that a genuine spirituality and the natural virtues be fostered, and that the womanly heart as well as "the head" be given sensitive guidance.[5]

Resistance to a sharp upgrading of the womanly role in the Church was indicated in the jingle recited on the margins of the Vatican II assembly (*congregatio* in the official Latin):

77

> Suenens said in the *congregatio*
> That it was time to end *segregatio.*
> Lest the bishops be churls,
> They should bring on the girls,
> E'en at the cost of some *admiratio.*

Inertia and jingles failed to block the way to change in a century when more and more women have won suffrage and equality with men in most areas of life. The Constitution on the Church, adopted by Vatican II as probably its greatest single work, pledged in Chapter IV on the laity: "There is therefore in Christ and in the Church no inequality on the basis of race or nationality, social condition or sex, because 'there is neither Jew nor Greek; there is neither bond nor free; there is neither male nor female. For you are all one in Christ Jesus' (Gal. 3:28; Col. 3:11)."[6]

The concessions by council, popes, cardinals, bishops and laymen came no sooner than necessary, for a demand for change was evident throughout the worlds of the 180,000 American Catholic nuns and of the 25 million lay women. Sometimes it was indicated only in a smiling remark. During a lecture visit to the campus of Misericordia College, Dallas, Pennsylvania, I was told by a sister there in the winter of 1965–66, "I hear that we American sisters are not well regarded in Rome, because we were the ones who educated most of the American bishops." The sister was commenting on the truism that America's Catholic hierarchy, as a rule, has not been distinguished for intellectuality.

Sometimes the call for change came from the top rank of the sisters' own organizations. Sister Mary Luke, the auditor who represented the American sisters at Vatican II, was quoted in the *Catholic Digest* of April, 1965, as listing two things her fellow sisters hoped for from the council, and thus from the current evolution in the Church:

1. Some representation for the sisters inside the Church bureaucracy which governs them (presumably the Roman congregations).

2. Some "reflection" of Vatican II's *aggiornamento* inside their lives: "the Resurrection, without forgetting the Crucifixion." As Sister saw it the latter often filled a nun's life and especially at the dramatic moment in which she entered her order. Some induction ceremonies, said Sister Mary Luke, were funereal rather than joyful, with novices sometimes required to affirm that: "I am accepting this world-despised, somber habit."

The same auditor for America's nuns said at a reception for the American bishops given by the Paulist Fathers in Rome on November 4, 1965, that America's sisters had to "find their own way to a wider openness to all things human." She said that such an evolution already was under way in "practical and far-reaching" adaptations, following the thought of Pope Paul "who stated in September (1965) that sisters have been marginal to contemporary society."[7]

Sister Bertrande Meyers, president of Missouri's Marillac College, and a member of the National Committee of the Sister Formation Conference, a major force for the updating of the United States Sisterhoods, listed in her *Sisters for the 21st Century*[8] what she called the desires and, bit by bit, the achievements of the majority of the United States nuns:

A new "horarium" to allow more time for study and for classroom preparation.

Fewer cooking, sewing, laundry and other household chores for each of the sisters in order to free them for additional professional reading.

More mental prayer, a minimum of vocal prayer, more variety and modernity in available spiritual reading.

Changes and even radical alterations in costumes drawn from earlier centuries and from other nations.

Remarks by Sister John Marie, superior of the Juniorate of the Sisters of St. Joseph in St. Louis, were even more pungent. She said that a root cause was that men, not women, drew up the basic Church laws governing the lives of sisters.[9]

"Should religious women unite to demand their rights of Holy Mother Church," said Sister John Marie, who was a professor of theology at Fontbonne College in St. Louis, "I think that our first request would be that we be treated as adults. We would ask that Canon 607 be abolished." That canon, she said, specified that sisters should not walk the streets alone. "Any prudent woman," the sister said, "whatever her state of life, will know that there are times and places when it is improper or inadvisable or socially unacceptable for her to go out unaccompanied. Could not sisters be trusted to make simple prudential judgments?"

Some long strides away from the ways of a centuries-old past were taken. Sister Patricia Jean, the educational assistant to the president of Loretto Heights College, Denver, was allowed, for instance, to set up housekeeping by herself in a two-room frame building near Antioch College where she took a course in administration, using a grant from the American Council on Education. She kept up a stream of memoranda back to her convent, reporting on the Antioch experiences. Finding anything revolutionary in the arrangement, she said, is, "I think, simply a matter of failing to treat Sisters as mature persons who can live apart from their community for nine months."[10]

Sister Mary Maurice of Mount Mercy College, Pittsburgh, was given an even greater concession. A biology professor, she was allowed to take a two-month cruise on a United States Navy vessel on a scientific mission in the waters of the Antarctic. In addition to the Navy crew and thirty male scientists, there was only one other woman aboard. Sister Mary Maurice was instructed to wear her habit as she walked up and down the gangplank on the two ends of the trip, but she was allowed to switch to heavy trousers and a jacket, as sea conditions indicated, after that. The nun was dispensed from Mass and the sacraments for the eight weeks.

The proposals and modifications were numerous, but were

they enough to meet the demands of the twentieth-century women clad in the medieval habits? Occasional expressions of indignation in articles in the Catholic press indicated that in the view of at least some of the nuns the changes were too few and slow. In the astonishingly frank "Sisters' Forum" of *The Catholic Reporter,* Sister M. Berchmans, of Wichita, Kansas, put these questions:

> Does it not seem paradoxical that at the Vatican Council, one sister was representing 180,000 women religious from the United States?
>
> Is it not odd that this one sister is ranked with those of other faiths, as an observer?
>
> Does it not seem strange amidst all the uproar about the habits, practices and rules of religious women that they have no part in the revision of Canon Law, the law that governs their lives?"[11]

Sister omitted the comment but the one nun, Sister Mary Luke, who had merely observer status while representing 180,000 American sisters was paralleled by more than 250 bishops and heads of religious orders drawn from the ranks of the 58,000 American priests. All of these 250 had votes. The priests thus had nearly 800 times the representation of the nuns, all of it in voting form, while the sisters—given one voice—had no ballots at all.

That nuns always will be patient with an ancient lot could not be assumed, as another remarkable contribution to the January 7, 1966, "Sisters' Forum" of *The Catholic Reporter* indicated. It took the form of a book review of *Asylums* by Erving Goffman.[12] The reviewer was Sister M. Aloysius Schaldenbrand. She praised author Goffman for "high moral passion" in a study "mainly of mental hospitals" but also of all other "total institutions: prisons, barracks, tuberculosis sanitaria, concentration camps, boarding schools, convents, and monasteries."

In all these "total institutions," whether mental asylums or convents, the same rules tend to apply. Sister M. Aloysius admiringly summed up the Goffman thesis: a small staff which seems "usually . . . condescending, high-handed and mean" faces a mass which is often "bitter, secretive and untrustworthy." To make the "mass" manageable the managers get them to break with their past, forbidding or limiting letters and callers, discouraging conversation about past circumstances, stripping the inmate of everything personal (from clothing to name), removing often even such liberties as the uninhibited right to a telephone call, a cigarette or even a glass of water, and finally invading "self territories" through such devices as the public confessions in monastic *culpa* (guilt) sessions.

Sister M. Aloysius invited convents to measure their own distance from Goffman's concept of the distressing "total institution" by answering one question: "Are [your] rules such that normal, twentieth-century adults find them embarrassing?" Her implication was strong that all too many would find themselves awkwardly close to the Goffman definition of an "asylum."

The anguish if not the active rebellion among some sisters as the ways of a medieval past collided with the philosophies of a bisexual modern world were reflected in still another contribution to the "Sisters' Forum."[13] A nun, this one writing anonymously, told of remarks by young sisters who felt their vocations in danger. The task of the letter writer was to dissuade them from leaving the convent. She cited various of the tormented remarks:

"When I think what I put my mother through to come—and what have I got to show for it? Twelve years of endurance, twelve years of frustration and, I'm afraid, less charity than twelve years ago."

"I'm not made of iron. I can only stand so much."

"In conscience, I do not feel I can continue to live this false, warped existence."

The Catholic Reporter headlined the letter "Confused sister asks question . . .," for the nun correspondent went on to say that one of the sisters she had counseled had refused to stay on in the order, and that her own thoughts were these:

Can we be certain that God wills us to spend a life of endurance when the world is waiting to hear the Gospel? Is it doctrine that a life lived under vows is more pleasing to God than a life of service? . . . It seems that a new community could be formed, following the guide lines of the Peace Corps. Sisters could volunteer for a minimum of two years from the established communities. This Sister Corps would save vocations, work toward its goal and, if and when the Sisters returned to their former communities, they would have much to share with them.

The Kansas City diocesan paper was sympathetic. "It seems to me," an editor wrote, "that there have been in recent years an unprecedented number of good Sisters leaving religious life because their community was for them more a hindrance than a help to Christian living. . . . Perhaps a new, rather flexible community to provide a chance for these Sisters, is needed."

The impact of a free, active, democratic century on the consecrated virgins of the Roman Catholic community could not help but have repercussions inside the minds and attitudes of inquiring laity, too, for one vast phase of the ferment among the nuns concerned them specifically as women, a condition shared with half the laity.

FIVE

Women
in "Their Place"

A priest in a lower-middle-class parish in the Queens section of New York City asked me to lecture one evening to his women's sodality. Typically, it was the clergyman who made the arrangements, but he withdrew to the wings of the auditorium stage as questions began. My topic had been the evolution. I had seen in thirteen years as a Vatican correspondent. The first demand astonished me.

"When will women be allowed to take a part in conducting religious services in the Catholic Church?"

Later, when the coffee hour began, the priest came back.

"We heard you clapping your hands," the woman chairman said cheerfully to him.

"You heard me wringing my hands," the priest replied with an unhappy half-smile.

The National Council of Catholic Women, the official Church organization for the distaff side, reported accurately in its 1962–64 biennial statement: "One of the most drastic changes is that of the modern woman. . . . She . . . must become personally involved [inside the Church]."

The ecclesiastical transformations touch women centrally. More often than they may realize the lay woman and the nun find themselves side by side in pressing for a fuller liturgical, legislative and supervisory role. In theory at least, Catholicism is prepared to grant these modifications. When Pope Paul VI appointed Mlle. Marie Monnet, of France, as history's first Catholic laywoman auditor at an ecumenical council, he explained his reasoning: "Because it is thanks to the common effort of all baptized that the council will have its fruits, we have wished that the laity be represented at the council, choosing men and women completely dedicated to the apostolate."

Mlle. Monnet was the president of the International Movement of Independent Social Interests, an association of Catholic Action workers who are not grouped inside other lay organizations. Daughter of a well-known cognac manufacturer, Mlle. Monnet was also the sister of Jean Monnet, the economist who had a large hand in shaping unification trends inside divided western Europe following World War II.

How deeply some Catholic women resented their marginal role was suggested in repeated articles by both nuns and lay women on the pages of Catholic publications.

Katherine Burton in her monthly column "Woman to Woman" in the Passionist Fathers' *The Sign,* returned time and again to the theme of liturgical emancipation for her sex. In January, 1965, she said sharply: "Long centuries ago, the desert fathers and Augustine and the rest put women definitely in their place, or anyway in a place. . . ."

In an earlier column, in November, 1964, Miss Burton had this tart observation: "In all the little pamphlets on how to be good and how not to be bad, in all the little sermons in print, I have never seen in the church rack one by Mary Daly or Rosemary Lauer or such talented women."

The January, 1965, column by Miss Burton struck a responsive chord at St. Margaret's Academy, Minneapolis. Sister Mary Micheas, writing from there, told *The Sign:*

Amen to Katherine Burton's "A Lament for Catholic Women."
. . . We have many distinguished Catholic laywomen who ought to
be present in some capacity at the [ecumenical] council. They
should be there by virtue of their love for the Church, their loyalty
to the Church, their intelligence about the Church. They should be
there because they, too, *are* the Church. Perhaps if articulate
women like Katherine Burton keep insisting on these facts, the
fourth and final session of Vatican Council II will open not only
the window (Pope John's metaphor) but some of the doors, and
the women will come marching in.[1]

Not only feminine voices were raised in favor of a wider-
door policy for ladies at the ecumenical council. Father
Donald R. Campion, a Jesuit, pondered the question in
America, in an October 31, 1964, "Letter from the Council."
He argued that the discussion of the schema on "The Church
in the Modern World" would "surely benefit from having
someone as informed as Lady Jackson (Barbara Ward)
speaking on our present capacity to abolish world poverty."

Lady Jackson was an economist dedicated to the proposi-
tion that the immense wealth of the North Atlantic nations
(notably of the United States) had to be shared more
generously with Latin America, Africa and Asia. She was a
candidate of many to be the first lay woman to speak at an
ecumenical council, but Vatican II, an innovator in so many
other regards, adjourned before taking the step. No woman,
nun or otherwise, has ever spoken in Catholicism's main
legislative assemblies, the periodic ecumenical councils.

Father Andrew Greeley, the Chicago sociologist, who has
been one of the most diligent students of evolving American
Catholicism, and even Pope John XXIII, were others who
were cited in the women's cause. Cecelia Wallace, of the
Centre of Ecumenical Studies of St. Michael's College at the
University of Toronto, wrote in the September, 1965, issue of
The Lamp that antifeminist ideas tracing back to Confucius
and Aristotle had to be eradicated from the modern world.
She added:

We are going to have to come to grips with a lot of worldwide attitudes dating from primitive times before we bring a satisfactory solution to this problem.

Fortunately, as Father Andrew Greeley . . . points out, the late Pope John in his encyclical "Peace on Earth" gave a strong endorsement of the feminist movement. He saw it as one of the great changes of modern times. "American Catholicism," states Father Greeley, "is simply unable to assimilate such a revolutionary concept." . . . There has not been and there is not now any Christian theology which fully recognizes woman's equality with man, although this is evolving for a number of reasons.

Support for the cause of women's ecclesiastical emancipation came from many countries. An example was an editorial in the early sixties in *The Clergy Bulletin,* the official publication of the association of Catholic priests of Bavaria and of the Palatinate in Germany. It commented about the function of women in the Church:

This question may not be answered in a negative mood only. The very fact of the extraordinary role of Mary in the history of salvation should make one ponder. Also the early Church knew how to avail itself of the services of women. In the days of the Apostles there were deaconesses, virgins and widows performing important tasks although the priesthood was not accessible to women.

In the history of the Church abbesses, erudite and pious nuns, also saintly wives and mothers, women of the nobility and those of lower social status, have exercised the greatest influence."

The attitudes against which Church feminists rebelled were often more apparent than the role they desired. The ecclesiastical "suffragettes" objected to old attitudes holding that women were inferior and, in some sense, not quite holy. Sister Albertus Magnus of Rosary College, River Forest, Illinois, made this point in *The Catholic Reporter.* She said that the Apocrypha and ancient Jewish law took the view that "woman, as woman, defiles the House of God." Sister's article was a good example of the way in which the feminist struggle has known no convent walls separating nuns and lay women in the common effort to achieve a better standing. She said:

> That the Catholic Church did not abandon these notions [of the Apocrypha and Jewish law] can be seen in the requirement for the "churching" of women [recently and not quite credibly explained as having quite other connotations]; in the very recently abrogated regulation that the priest, and not the sacristan even though she be a consecrated virgin, should wash the communion linens; in the antiphon chanted daily by sisters who recite the Little Office: "After childbirth, O Virgin, thou still didst remain *undefiled*. . . ." Finally it can be seen in the rules which permit any male child over six to serve at the altar, while no girl or woman, however worthy, can enter into the sanctuary during a liturgical service. She may assist at the sacred mysteries, so long as she preserves due silence, neither serving at the altar nor reading the epistle nor acting as a commentator in the revised liturgy. Whatever else Vatican II did or did not do, it did not recognize women as belonging in all things equally with men to the People of God.[3]

Jewish law, Sister Albertus Magnus pointed out, "required abstention from religious services immediately after intercourse, demanded the ceremonial purification of women after menstruation and childbirth [and] relegated women to the outer courts of the temple." With different rules and emphases there were signs nonetheless that Christianity and Catholicism "did not entirely" give up this attitude of taboo with regard to various aspects of woman's nature.

Katherine Burton used her *The Sign* magazine column, "Woman to Woman," in September, 1965, to make a similar protest against inherited Church views about womenfolk. St. Thomas Aquinas, she said, was the author of one comment on womankind to which she heartily objected, that "girl children are accidents of creation caused [St. Thomas] surmised, by an unexpected warm wind from the Adriatic."

Mrs. Burton drew heavily in that column on research done for *The Lamp* by Dr. Rosemary Lauer, another indignant feminist. Dr. Lauer's article, "Are Women Less 'Equal' than Men?" came up with these antifemale gems from Church history:

St. John Damascene said that woman was a hideous tapeworm, the front door to Hell. St. Gregory the Great affirmed that women were useful for two purposes: motherhood and harlotry. Hugo of Pisa said that women were all right for looking after men in the latter's old age.

The effort to find a better and more correct place for women was by no means merely a Catholic phenomenon. The Protestant churches and Judaism grappled with the question too. Bishop James A. Pike, of the Episcopal Church of the United States, pointed out in the mid-sixties that the Church of Sweden, the Presbyterians, the Methodists, the Disciples of Christ and the United Church of Christ all had ordained women as full clergymen. He tried to give ordination to Miss Phyllis Edwards as an episcopal deacon to assist at Holy Communion and in the administration of sacraments to the sick but, after protests, desisted.

The repercussions inside Judaism were reflected in an article in *The United Synagogue Review*, by Rabbi Howard Singer, the spiritual leader of the Laurelton Jewish Center in Queens, New York. He said that some women objected to "the low opinion [the Jewish religion] has of women," and wanted equality. Some ladies, he said, resented the ancient Jewish custom requiring women to sit behind a curtain in a separate part of the synagogue. Rabbi Singer made three comments in reply: The ancient Christian fathers, in his view, went well beyond the Jews of antiquity in antifeminism. A "separate" status does not necessarily mean an "inferior" one. Caution about woman and her beauty is by no means inappropriate in a place of prayer.

The rabbi made these points:

Separation [of men and women in a place of religious devotion] seems to imply inferiority to us, but we look at it with the eyes of moderns. The truth is that the ancients separated the sexes simply because they were far more serious about chastity for the unmarried, and fidelity for the married, than we are. I suspect that, in some ways, they were more realistic. They freely admitted what we are too inhibited to concede, that a normal man may have some difficulty concentrating on prayers when an attractive young woman in a revealing gown sits beside him. For them the solution was simple: in the synagogue put men on one side of a curtain, women on the other. Outside the synagogue you don't . . . "gaze too long at their beauty." In a word, you put up barriers quite deliberately. The reason is not because they are inferior, but because they are female. . . .[4]

Some of those taking part in the great debate had clear ideas of the greater role they wished for women in the Church. St. Joan's International Alliance, a movement which originated in England as a battler for equality for women in both civil and Church life, petitioned the papal commission for the revision of Canon Law to make these changes: an elimination of the requirement that women cover their heads in church; permission to women to preach wherever laymen obtain that right.[5]

Sister William of the Monastery of the Poor Clares of Chicago told *The Catholic Reporter* on January 7, 1966, that woman's influence in the Church was "minimal" in her opinion. She added that "whether or not woman serves Mass or reads the lessons is not important to me," but she did yearn for a Church in which the "ethical and spiritual influence" of women could be felt.

"If women," said the sister with the man's name, "were consulted and their advice sought on any and all levels of Church life, we would end up with . . . a Church we could more easily call 'Mother.' . . ."

In battle after battle in the pages of the religious publications, in Church conventions and in private conversations, nuns and laywomen marched side by side in the cause of feminine emancipation. Sometimes their revolt was complicated, however, by reactions against one another. An example was Mrs. Frances S. Conway's letter from Cameron, Missouri, to *The Catholic Reporter* on September 17, 1965. She objected to an article in an earlier issue of the weekly contributed by Sister M. Aloysius Schaldenbrand on the virtues of the permanently unmarried state. Said Mrs. Conway, a married laywoman and unashamed of it: "I'm tired! I'm tired of articles aimed at—not me, certainly!—like 'The Virgin Witness'—wherein Sister . . . lost me along the way —me, this poor, tired, benighted, uneducated member of the laity. I wonder if she didn't lose herself along the way, just a little. . . ."

The consecrated virgin versus the married laywoman, the long repressed woman in the Church versus the man— feminine emancipation was only one of many revolutions and evolutions urging the laity forward toward a new position inside the Church as the twentieth century's final third began.

SIX

Gales through
the Open Window

A chat one day in a village behind Mount Vesuvius in Italy summed up the tangled emotions in an era of liturgical and even, in a sense, doctrinal change. The village was named after Saint Philomena, a virgin of the ancient Roman world who was still honored in the stained glass of an apse window in our local church in Great Neck, Long Island, in the final half decade of the sixties.

Saint Philomena had enjoyed a phenomenal cult, especially, for some reason, inside the motion picture colony in Hollywood. She was said to be a woman of piety whose life was in some way identified with the sea. She was known as a miracle worker. Her cult had spread in the early 1800s when a Vesuvius pastor brought her bones from recently rediscovered catacombs in Rome. That, in any case, was the Saint Philomena story as it was told until the final years of the fifties. Then the historical section of the Congregation of Rites affirmed that Saint Philomena had never existed. Pieces of her broken coffin slab had been fitted together in the wrong sequence when diggers in the ancient burial ground had unearthed her remains. An anchor had been misinterpreted as a sign of some association with the sea. There was no evidence of special sanctity. The shrine behind Vesuvius was ordered to remove "Philomena's" masked and clothed bones from the altar crystal casket in which they had been displayed for nearly two centuries. I went to the town and found chaos. The unhappy pastor had done nothing to close a center which had become the goal of international pilgrimages. Townspeople muttered that they would never allow the banishment of "their saint." I eyed sullen bystanders at a sidewalk café as I entered the shrine church. The Communist mayor, interviewed inside his cluttered office-home, told me that although he was a nonbeliever he would lead a popular uprising rather than let the priest remove "Philomena's" remains. It was not just that the shrine had become the village's main industry, the Communist said. Townspeople had given their hearts and trust to "Philomena."

"It was the Church which brought her," the agnostic mayor said. "It is the Church's responsibility now. It is too late to take her away."

The neat, scholarly, becassocked monsignor in the historical section on Pius XII Square in front of St. Peter's in Rome was unmoved by such arguments. Many ordinary folk had been buried in catacombs and had been mistaken later as martyrs and saints, he said. The truth, and not pious misapprehensions, had to be served.

My sympathies were with the monsignor. Pious error is nonetheless error, but the shock in Philomena's town and in Catholic parishes around the world was severe.

Thus a further dimension was added in the second half of the twentieth century to the ferment which was fostering a reexamination of all traditions, including that of a submerged laity. This added dimension was that of change inside the cult, the understanding of the faith and the clergy itself. Here, too, the pages of the Catholic press, once static and content, provided myriad examples.

For one thing, the Church publications reflected a revolution in Biblical interpretation. On one of many visits I paid in the middle fifties to Pius XII's private secretary, the Jesuit Father Leiber, the priest told me that the new Biblical interpretations, especially in Germany, were occupying the pontiff's distressed attention.

Pius XII himself in 1943, and Pius XI before him, had opened the way for a Catholic revolution in understanding of the Bible. Pius XII had given broad authorization to Catholic scholars to use the tools of other sciences—of archaeology, of ethnology, of historical research, of language and literary study—to pry out the gems of old wisdom from the symbolisms of the Bible. With that edict, a school of Catholic fundamentalist, literalist Bible interpretation withered. Cardinal Augustine Bea, Pius XII's confessor and the ecumenical council's main sponsor of interfaith reconciliation, discussed aspects of his experiences with me on several occasions. When Protestant Biblical scholars had asked the Vatican to send Catholic spokesmen to one of their conventions, Pius XI turned his back on centuries of isolation by saying, in effect, to the future Cardinal Bea, head of Rome's Catholic Bible Institute: "Go, and take others with you. Just be sure they know their subject."

The cardinal-to-be made such a hit as a frank and open seeker after elusive Biblical truth that he was invited to give the closing address. One set of walls separating Catholics and Protestants and dividing both of them from a better comprehension of Bible mysteries had been removed.

To some extent what Catholic and Protestant scholars began to share was a mutual confession of their difficulty in interpreting much of Sacred Scripture. Soon religious publications were crowded with Biblical puzzles which were bound to bewilder the faithful. Examples were numerous:

In November, 1965, *The Sign* published a letter challenging the editor to give the location of Heaven. "It must be a physical place, since the Blessed Mother," said the letter writer, "was taken up in body and soul [in the Assumption, a dogma proclaimed before a world assemblage of the Catholic hierarchy by Pius XII in the 1950 Holy Year]."

The Sign answered that "maybe the resurrected Christ and His Mother are here on earth" for it is "impossible to conceive of them not being somewhere." If the "new theology" could have given a better answer, an explanation perhaps that some mysteries of faith are beyond man's mind, *The Sign's* writer had no such reply to offer.

The National Council of Catholic Men in 1965 published a copyrighted pamphlet, *The Bible and the Laity,* designed to respond to some of the Scriptural inquiries. Is it true, the hierarchy's laity agency asked, for instance, that the waters lifted Noah and the ark higher and higher until the loftiest peaks "everywhere under the heaven were covered"?[1] The NCCM answer: No, even though some scientists report a great Tigris-Euphrates flood prior to 4000 B.C., the Bible tells "the story of baptism"; it recounts "salvation history" and "not geology or oceanography." The Tigris-Euphrates flood in point of fact "did not cover the entire earth."

In article after article and in letters to editors, the Catholic publications brought further questions before their readers:

Could a fisherman of such little apparent culture as that of St. Peter (his Galilean accent gave him away at Christ's Passion) have written the epistles in the good Greek which is attributed to him? The answer, in the Rev. Dr. Joseph J. Tennant's column in the September 23, 1965, *The Long Island Catholic:* "No one knows even the slightest thing about the personal activities of St. Peter except the few bits of information . . . in the Gospels and the Acts of the Apostles." Did he study Greek? No one knows, but "it must be remembered that he was a Jew, and even uneducated Jews are not incapable of learning languages."

Are the Gospels "interconnecting biographies of Jesus

Christ and nothing more"? The Rev. Dr. Martin J. Healy raised that question in *The Long Island Catholic* on April 8, 1965, and gave this answer: No, God's truth must be sought beneath the accounts given by Matthew, Mark, Luke, and John. From earliest Christian history writers have failed to patch the Gospels together into one good single story of Christ and have found that no two accounts of the Resurrection agree on details. "It is not that they contradict one another, but they seem to be telling of the resurrection of four different men." Father Healy added this observation: it is "an astonishing fact" that the feeding of the five thousand with the loaves and fishes is the only one of thirty-six miracles which is reported by each of the evangelists. Three repeat the story of eleven of the miracles. Two tell of another five. Nineteen of the supernatural phenomena, more than half, are recorded only once.

What is to be made of the Genesis idea that the firmament was an inverted bowl with the edges touching the earth, and with the sun, moon and stars fastened to the inner side, while rain poured through "windows"? Bishop Charles P. Greco, supreme chaplain for the Knights of Columbus, made his reply in a 1965 "religious outline" published by the K of C. This "unscientific and unreal" conception of the world, he wrote to K of C members, was a "primitive" way of looking at the universe and was "entirely incidental to [the inspired writer's] main story." It was no more of a "misstatement" than references nowadays to "sunsets."

Finally, what about odd parallels between the stories of Genesis and the tales told by other faiths in the ancient Mediterranean world? What about evident errors in the Old Testament? Father Carroll Stuhlmueller, author of *The Prophets and the Word of God,* responded in an interview in *The Sign,* in April, 1965. On "errors" he conceded that calling Nebuchadnezzar king of the Assyrians in the Book of Judith was like referring to "Stalin as the former dictator of

Nazi Germany." Even so, Father Stuhlmueller said, the point of the account is evident and accurate, that when Israel is faithful to God she vanquishes oppressors whether they be Stalins or Hitlers. As for startling parallels, Father Stuhlmueller added, there are the flood stories in the literature of Assyria, Babylon, Sumeria and Ugarit, and Middle Eastern tales of ancestors who far outlived Methuselah (including a Sumerian king listing which described eight men reigning for 241,000 years!). Neighbors of the ancient Jews, as Father Stuhlmueller added, told further of "a certain 'Etana, a shepherd, who ascended into heaven.'" The *Passionist* magazine, in a caption, gave the interview's moral: "A strictly literal interpretation [of the Bible] often does not rest upon faith, but upon ignorance and error."

Revolutionary was the word for the new Biblical understandings, and even liberal churchmen such as Montreal's Cardinal Paul Emile Léger were concerned about consequences among the faithful. As he said in Rome on June 16, 1964: "No good can come from continual discussion at the popular level of the latest theories and interpretations of the Scripture. This must not be interpreted to mean that I do not wish to encourage . . . the work of those who give their lives to the Word of God. On the contrary these devoted men deserve our thanks and praise, and their work must be allowed to progress serenely on its way. But I would emphasize it is a work for experts who must be freed from pressures which might come either from the abuse of authority or from those who seek spectacular results."

Whatever the cardinal's concern, the studies of the scholars continued to filter down into parish lay discussion groups, into parochial school textbooks, into occasional local sermons. One more force for change was agitating the once quiet world of the layman.

Side by side with the intellectual waves stirred by the Bible inquiries, came others from the seminaries, from the monasteries and from rectories as the present and future clergy reacted in their turn to an era of reevaluations and of new directions.

In most corners of the Catholic world there was a shortage of vocations. Graduation classes from the seminaries were not keeping up with the population growth and the expansion of the laity. An average of about one priest to 1,000 Catholics is considered normal in Europe, but Venezuela, in one illustration of the crisis, had only one clergyman for 5,000. The American Catholic Church, with a priest for every 770 members, had a rather high clerical proportion, but it could not ignore next-door Latin America. Baltimore's cardinal, Lawrence Shehan, had one word for the vocation need: "Desperate."

One reason was the vast loss of vocations inside the seminaries. Father John T. Nolan commented in *The Catholic Reporter* that "it is common knowledge that 80 to 90 percent of the boys who enter a minor seminary do not continue the full twelve years to ordination."[2] A copyrighted analysis of seminary fallout rates done in 1965 by Father Cornelius M. Cuyler, of Catonsville, Maryland, included startling statistics. Father Cuyler studied records of thousands of seminarians at scores of minor and major seminaries of the United States over a thirty-year period and came up with these observations:

Out of a mass of 29,773 boys of the age of fourteen who entered sixty-eight high school seminaries in the United States between 1935 and 1952 only 4,954—one sixth—were in due time ordained priests.

Many dropped out during the critical summer between the end of the college seminary and the beginning of the last four postgraduate years of theological study. Just over one third quit during that decisive trimester. Still more disturbing was the fact that a substantial, and rising, number entered "theology" and then stepped aside before advancing to the altar. The preparatory seminary classes which started in the 1935–39 period lost 6.8 percent of their members during theology, while the last group studied, that of 1950–52, suffered a dropout rate of 19.7 percent, three times higher, during the final four years.

Seminaries which took boys at the college freshman level, at eighteen years of age, reported a similar experience. Schools for the priesthood were multiplying. Starting classes were bigger. But the dropout rate was climbing so sharply that Father Cuyler saw evidence that the number of priests actually ordained might settle down to a dead level of the same number each year. That would be a sharp setback for a Church with a steadily growing membership. Seventy-three seminaries which started at the college level told Father Cuyler that between 1935 and 1956 only 49.3 percent of the eighteen-year-old beginners went on to be ordained eight years later. For each man who persevered, one withdrew. And the success curve was abruptly down. Between 1935 and 1939, 57.9 percent of those who started seminary studies at eighteen became priests. Between 1955 and 1956, two decades later, only 41.9 percent went through to ordination.

What was wrong? Father Cuyler speculated that the rise in the theology dropout rate in the twenty-two to twenty-six age group might mean that "the world's attractions [were] affecting those old enough to realize what they are"—an apparent reference to the priest's burden of celibacy. He added: "Could it possibly be that our teaching is dry and uninspired or that our rules and regulations are, at times, what they have been called, picayune? Maybe some seminary windows should be opened wider."

By the middle sixties a phrase of Father Andrew Greeley, a sociologist contributor to the Jesuits' *America,* had become a cliché: the Catholic seminaries of the United States were chockablock with "a new breed," a generation which wanted explanations instead of the unsupported word of authority, students for the priesthood who wanted to learn how to minister to distracted modern man in a twentieth-century way, and not with the formulas of a half-forgotten past. Mixed in too, no doubt, was what Maryland's Cardinal Shehan nervously observed, the influence of the times: "an unprecedented prosperity, material allurements, permissiveness in families, a lack of discipline." The times were too easy, too enticing.

There were at least two schools among the older clergy concerning this "new breed." Father Greeley, who coined the name for the new-type seminarian, was, for his part, dubious about them. He said in *America* on May 22, 1965: "[There is] almost total misunderstanding between them and their predecessors, a misunderstanding perhaps more acute than has ever before separated an older and a younger generation." He continued:

> The older generation interprets the constant questioning of established traditions, the incessant demand for explanation, the persistent and often apparently unreasonable criticism as being signs of revolt. But this revolt is one that can neither describe what it opposes nor make clear what it wants to substitute for the present order of the Church and of society. Superiors, parents, teachers, advisors, all of us find it exceedingly difficult to communicate with these young people.

This point inspired one further:

> New breeders seem to be manic-depressives. . . . It seems to me that in their lives there are, indeed, just too many "great, big hairy deals. . . ." Many of them leave college or the seminary because as they say 'I will be destroyed if I stay here any longer.' Perhaps indeed they will be destroyed, though one wonders if the problem may be more simply that they lack the emotional fortitude to stick out a difficult situation.

The other side of the new breed coin was turned up by Father Robert L. Richard, also writing in *America:*

The kind of priest this young man [the new breeder] wants to be clearly reflects the best present-day theological and philosophical thought, . . . a historically critical repossession of the New Testament message and values, . . . a concern for the meaningful and the timely over and above the merely right and true. . . . Unlike so many of his elders (including unfortunately too large a number of his professors) he sees clearly that a 20-hour work week with maybe twice that for television is simply a scandal. . . . He looks forward to his ordination as a consecration to service, not *otium cum dignitate* [lazy dignity]. . . . If allowed he takes part in civil rights discussions, even demonstrations. He works with the poor and suffering, in schools, hospitals, social projects, and from door to door. He engages enthusiastically in the present-day ecumenical dialogue."[4]

Another with a good word for this generation of seminarians, however ravaged they might be by a high dropout rate, was Father Joseph Buckley, the general of the Marist Fathers, of St. Paul, Minnesota. Talking to the ecumenical council in St. Peter's on November 11, 1964, he said: "Some superiors are always talking about the crisis in obedience. My opinion is that the crisis is with the superiors, not with the subjects. The truth is that today's young people don't swallow archaic formulas like 'the will of the superior is exactly the same as the will of God.' "

Whatever the reason—a willful, spoiled generation lured by the pleasures of an unprecedented comfortable era, or a rigid old seminary system unable to profit quickly from the legacy of Pope John and of Vatican Council II—the need for a wholesale review of seminary instruction and customs was evident. Father William J. Gibbons, a Fordham University lecturer on demography, told the National Catholic Welfare Conference News Service in November, 1963: "The graduates [of the seminaries] must have an intellectual preparation, training and professional outlook as expected of them by educated men both in and outside the Church."

What would that mean? Father John B. Sheerin, editor of

The Catholic World, suggested one omission to me: "I know of no seminary where they read newspapers."

The type of seminary which might be on its way out was indicated by a December 17, 1965, article in *The Catholic Reporter,* describing a change of administration at Chicago's St. Mary of the Lake Seminary. The new archbishop, John P. Cody, a member of the hierarchy's postconciliar commission on seminary reform, found fifty-nine rules in effect including these:

A seminarian was expected to excuse himself immediately but politely from the company of any lay visitors he might encounter about the grounds.

None but relatives might visit students in the seminary, and only on Sunday.

Walks with visiting relatives through the grounds were not allowed, nor was there any lounge which could be used for conversation. All encounters with visitors had to be inside seminary classrooms.

The seminary's collection of novels was under lock and key in the library. Most periodicals were banned. Seminarians were not allowed to visit the rooms of one another.

Students of St. Mary of the Lake told *Commonweal* in 1964 that they had taken a poll among Chicago priests and found that 58 percent of the graduate churchmen complained that their seminary life had hindered rather than helped relationships later with the laity. Ninety percent of those queried said that they felt that their knowledge of psychology was inadequate.

The new archbishop changed rectors and added an assistant director of the seminary, Father John Gorman, who was just finishing work for a doctorate in psychology. The forty-year-old rule book, drawn up by Cardinal George Mundelein, was revised to allow seminarians to leave the grounds once a week, on Thursday. It was altered also to permit more periodicals, to allow freer use of television and to authorize visits back and forth among the student rooms.

As the sixties drew on, few failed to see the need for more scholarly inquiry into the elusive meaning of Scripture and for drastic revisions in seminary courses and customs in order to graduate a clergy able to speak to an instructed modern generation. Therein lay the answer to much of the future, but meanwhile an even more immediate crisis concerned the core of the American Catholic Church—the 240 bishops and the 58,000 priests.

SEVEN

The Crisis of the Clergy

How deeply the American democratic spirit had penetrated into the priests of the United States was brought home at the first international convention of the Catholic press to be held in the United States. It was at the luxurious Waldorf-Astoria Hotel in New York in 1965. I was asked to chair an opening panel discussion on the issue of freedom versus obedience. My two panelists were New Hampshire's modern and courageous bishop, Ernest Primeau, who was mentioned as a possible future cardinal of his native Chicago, and Father Roberto Tucci, son of an Anglican-raised mother, and editor of the pope's special monthly magazine, *Civiltà Cattolica*, in Rome.

It seemed to me that my role as a layman newsman was simply symbolic and that my task was to turn the microphone over as quickly as possible to the two eminent spokesmen for Church leadership. I tried to say as little as possible and to stick to the obvious. I began: "The problem of authority and freedom must be as old as man. It is interesting that the very first citation on page one of *Bartlett's Quotations,* one of the most basic books of an English language library, is on the subject of authority. *Bartlett's* is chronologically arranged. The opening words are from 'The Instruction of Ptahhotep' in 2765 B.C. They read: 'To resist him that is set in authority is evil.' "

My intention was to next dig a few hundred pages deeper into *Bartlett's* to come up with some equally extreme tributes to liberty and freedom, but to my astonishment I had already lost part of my audience. Two priests in the front row were shaking their heads.

Throughout the American Catholic priesthood of the middle sixties there were freshets of renovation. Curates lamented that they had to wait twenty and twenty-five years in archdioceses like that of New York's Francis Cardinal Spellman before they could hope for a parish of their own. Some priests wondered about the wisdom of the Latin-rite ban which denied matrimony to the overwhelming share of the Roman Catholic priesthood of the world. Some talked privately of a retirement age for pastors and bishops, and of the election rather than the nomination of bishops. Many felt frustrated about limitations, preventing them from talking frankly to their pastors and to diocesan leaders.

It was scarcely surprising that so much should be opened for reconsideration, for the American bishops themselves had set the example at the 1962–65 ecumenical council in Rome. When conservatives in the largely Italian Curia of the papacy had passed the word in 1962 that they did not want any national hierarchy to caucus, the American prelates were astounded. Bishop Primeau, the member of my Waldorf-Astoria panel, and a veteran of years of life in Rome, was unimpressed. He could see no good reason why national groupings should not assemble nor, indeed, could he see why liaisons should not be set up between the various national bodies. By the time he finished doing something about it, the American hierarchy was meeting in Rome, not annually, as had been their custom in the States, but weekly; with Bishop Primeau doing much of the negotiating, formal ties were in effect with twenty other national hierarchies. The result was that when a critical election was held for key council offices the agreed slate of the twenty, including many Americans, won in a landslide. It was not the way Curia conservatives had planned it, and it helped assure liberal victories in the council pronouncements.

The same spirit of 1776 was behind one of the most dramatic events of four-year Vatican II. When 200 to 300 conservatives blocked consideration of a religious freedom declaration in the fall of 1964, two American clergymen strode out on the council floor opposite the statue of St. Peter inside the great Vatican Basilica. They protested so furiously that a victory for the historically significant document was assured at the closing session a year later.

The two that day were a Maryland Jesuit, Father John Courtney Murray, who had written much of the religious liberty statement, injecting into it the convictions of the toler-ant plural American society. The other was the customarily withdrawn and studious cardinal of Chicago, Albert Gregory Meyer. Friends of Father Murray were afraid that the ashen-faced priest would have a heart attack. The Marylander promised to go home to bed, but he stayed instead until nightfall, making sure that the newsmen of the world got the full story on how a minority of only about a fifth had post-poned, if not killed, the tolerance decree.

"It's scandalous! It's scandalous!" the Chicago cardinal objected at the dais of the council presidents.

Scores of the other American bishops joined Father Murray and Cardinal Meyer within moments. A junior member of the American hierarchy asked for paper, and someone borrowed a sheaf from the few newsmen present. "Urgently, more urgently, most urgently, we appeal to the Holy Father," someone scribbled in Latin. An Irish-Ameri-can priest ran off fifty copies on the Xerox machine in the office of the council's highly conservative secretary general, Archbishop Pericle Felici. Moments later 441 signatures of bishops were on the protest. Those who were present noticed the nervousness of old prelates at the council presidency.

"But it wasn't a revolt," one of those involved explained later. "There wasn't any walkout. That would have been a revolt."

It also would have been the front door to schism, the most dreaded of evils plaguing the life of the Church.

If it was not revolt, it did show the change which occurred in the American hierarchy during the four Rome years. Cardinal Spellman told friends that attending the council was like going back to school again, listening to an ocean of possible adaptations to a new world. Many of the American bishops had arrived in Rome in 1962 with the pages of the schemata, the council documents, still uncut. Neither they nor their aides had bothered to check into the matters on which they would be asked to speak and vote. After generations of isolated papal control, the habit of debate and even of fresh study had faded. By the time the council neared its end such a great leader of the liberal wing of American Catholicism as Archbishop Paul J. Hallinan (an open-minded ex-chaplain of the Newman Club movement on nonsectarian university campuses) told me: "My doctor won't let me attend more than half the sessions so I just pick out the ones where they vote!"

The archbishop had heard all he needed of the conservative-liberal clash by then. What he wanted was to make sure that his one small vote, one-twentieth of one percent of the council total, would weigh however lightly on the progressive side where he could almost invariably be found.

As it turned out, revolts or near-revolts, whatever you may call them, such as those of Bishop Primeau and of Father Murray and Cardinal Meyer, had their effect. Ten to one majorities supported most proposals for adaptation and evolution.

The American hierarchy in 1965, according to private estimates in the corridors of the National Catholic Welfare Conference (the American Catholic national headquarters) in Washington, could be appraised this way:

> Highly conservative, 125
> Moderates and middle-of-the-roaders, 75
> Liberals, reformers, progressives, 75

Liberals had the majority if they managed to swing practically all the uncommitted and the undecided, but conservatives could put drags on change quite easily and, especially, inside their own dioceses.

Editors and priests interviewed across the country agreed generally on who were the liberal leaders in the middle sixties. Their lists included these:

Cardinal Joseph Elmer Ritter, of St. Louis, an Indianan born in 1892, and thus already in his seventies. An unpretentious man, he took a strong stand on Negro rights just after World War II, desegregating his parochial schools years before the Supreme Court decision which imposed such a policy. At the council he was in a minority of the American hierarchy campaigning for large shifts of power from the Vatican to the local national conferences of bishops, a democratizing measure.

Cardinal Richard Cushing, of Boston, a generous, priestly man so unconcerned about "dignity" that he would pose for news photographers swapping and wearing the flowered hat of a plump old woman in Boston's city home for the aged. A reporter cannot forget an interview with the New England cardinal in Rome in the late fifties.

"How long will you be here?" I said, trying to get a conversation going.

"A week if they don't kick me out before then."

Cardinal-kicking is not a latter-day sport in Rome, nor is it even mentionable in a city of solemnly formal ways, but cheerless gravity was not one of the long suits of the wry, humble, kindly and often wise Bostonian.

The one caveat some had about listing Cardinal Cushing was that he stayed away from a large share of the ecumenical council sessions, bored with the endless chatter in Latin, and thus omitting the support he could have given the liberals. Boston friends quoted him on the eve of the council as he arranged for a large cash donation for the Vatican: "I'll just say, 'Holy Father, here's the gift of the good people of Boston, and now can I go home?' "

Cardinal Lawrence J. Shehan, of Baltimore, an advocate of better relations with other faiths.

Archbishop Hallinan. One of the many priests and editors who mentioned him added his own definition of a Church liberal: "Someone who realizes that the Church is Christ's eternal presence in society, and at the same time understands our present-day life in all its sociological, economic and political make-up. The liberal is not bound to the old ways which were appropriate in another era. He sees to it that the Church makes contact with society as it is now."

Archbishop John Francis Dearden, of Detroit. In the spring of 1965 he was one of the first to summon a little council of his own diocese (80 priests and 120 laymen), thus repeating the democratic Rome experience on the level of his own see. When the idea was broached to use Negro spirituals and modern music in Catholic worship, the prelate was willing to mull it over.

Archbishop John Patrick Cody, of Chicago.

Bishop John J. Wright, of Pittsburgh, a brilliant son of a poor Massachusetts family, and a graduate of the classics-centered Boston Latin School. He was so sensitive to change that he feared that an aggressive, articulate, scholarly laity might take the teaching function away from the clergy and

109

hierarchy, leaving them merely as the leaders of divine worship. He opposed that but welcomed laymen into a share of the liturgical and teaching role.

Auxiliary Bishop James P. Shannon, of St. Paul, former president of St. Thomas College, and publisher of *The Catholic Digest,* one of the most widely circulated American Catholic periodicals.

Bishop Primeau, of New Hampshire, the council "rebel."

Bishop Charles Herman Helmsing, of Kansas City, one of the first to shut down a slum area parochial school on the grounds that Catholics ought not to maintain instructional centers providing a low-grade education. He was sponsor, too, of *The National Catholic Reporter,* a modern-minded foe of the time-honored clerical habit of secrecy.

Bishop Charles A. Buswell, of Pueblo, Colorado.

Archbishop Robert Emmet Lucey, of San Antonio, Texas, and

Bishop Stephen A. Leven, Lucey's auxiliary.

Bishop Victor Reed, of Oklahoma City.

Bishop Robert E. Tracy, of Baton Rouge, a battler against racism.

Bishop John King Mussio, of Steubenville, Ohio.

Below the level of the hierarchy these names were often mentioned: Father Theodore M. Hesburgh, president of Notre Dame University; Father John Courtney Murray; Monsignor Francis J. Lally, editor of *The Pilot,* of Boston; Father Raymond T. Bosler, editor of *The Criterion,* of Indianapolis; Father Joseph Connelly of the Baltimore *Catholic Review;* Father Ed Flannery of the Providence, Rhode Island, *Visitor;* Father Frederick R. McManus, past president of the American Catholic Liturgical Conference; Father Gerard S. Sloyan, liturgist and head of the religious education department at the Catholic University of America in Washington; Father Godfrey Leo Diekmann, editor of *Worship;* and Father John L. McKenzie, archaeologist and past president of the Catholic Biblical Association.

The ranks of the liberals shifted issue to issue but, by and large, these were their objectives:

A modernization of the liturgy to make it comprehensible, if not at first glance, at least after short study.

An open-door policy with regard to joint ventures and exchanges of ideas with Protestants, Jews, the nonspiritual, the atheists and just about everybody.

A rollback of an all-encompassing clericalism in Church leadership and policy making, and a sharing of responsibility down the line from pope to bishop to pastor to curate and to layman.

An educated and active laity.

A church taking part in its community's life, and not locked inside forbidding walls.

Conservatives tended to rally around New York's Cardinal Spellman and his protégé, Cardinal J. Francis A. McIntyre, of Los Angeles, two prelates heavy with seniority in the American hierarchy.

"Cardinal Spellman," one of the prelate's close aides expressed it, "would be likely to sum up his own view in sporting terms: 'don't break up a winning team.'" The cardinal, in his seventies, remembered the pious, separate Catholic world of before World War I, a community which had won its long fight to prove its patriotism inside America, a society of simple devotions and of few ponderings either about the nature of the Church or about the future of America. In the late sixties he still saw crowded Communion rails inside dark turn-of-the-century churches which had been built by poor immigrants. He remembered much good in the past and deplored drifts in the present. He was content to keep things about as they were. Scores of other elderly, conservative bishops agreed.

Cardinal McIntyre, a Wall Street broker until he was twenty-nine, served Cardinal Spellman for years in New York as chancellor or business manager, laying the financial groundwork for projects of construction of schools, asylums and hospitals, and preparing himself for his own leadership of Los Angeles where he regularly added a new Catholic institution each week. The cardinal years later was remembered at the New York chancery as a priest who was always cheerfully ready to take a late-night sick call, and as a diocesan "business" man who often could be seen walking visitors across traffic-choked Madison Avenue from his chancery building to St. Patrick's Cathedral, on his way to the confessional boxes of St. Patrick's to hear the caller's story in sacramental fashion and to give absolution. He was a priest, said a friend, "who in any other century would have been great" but who, in the late twentieth century, found the Negro protest hard to grasp and to accept.

Conservative bishops such as Cardinal McIntyre understandably found it hard to comprehend clerics like twenty-nine-year-old Father William Henry DuBay, a curate in an 80 percent Negro parish in Los Angeles, who wrote a letter to Pope Paul VI and published a book setting forth two propositions: that the cardinal should be removed for failing to give moral leadership to the Negro drive for equal rights, and that a labor union should be set up for priests.

The idea that priests, men who have given themselves to God and to the successors of Christ's apostles in a spirit of self-abnegation and obedience, should organize like bricklayers was hard even for many liberals to comprehend, but Father Francis Canavan reported significantly in *America,* in the first weeks of 1966, that priests whom he polled on a not-for-attribution basis made these comments:

Many favored the establishment of some sort of grievance machinery so that a priest could take his complaints to a personnel director appointed by the bishop or to a diocesan court of rights, with appeal perhaps to another diocese. The priests, Father Canavan found, felt that they had no voice in policy decisions on the diocesan or even on lower levels. They wanted one. They suffered from the lack of a voice in policy questions and from a lack of recourse in the face of decisions which they considered mistaken.

Young Father DuBay, said the associate editor of *America,* "probably does not have a shining future in the church" and certainly will never sit across the table from his cardinal as "president of Local 105 of the International Union of Pastors and Curates, AFL–CIO."

But, he added, Church reformers would do well to study how modern constitutional monarchies manage to reconcile authority with protections against "arbitrariness in [the] administrative bureaucracies."

Mental breakdowns, alcoholism, sudden marriages and abandonment of the priesthood and even of the Church, periodically were reported, though traditional reticence drew the curtain in front of many such cases. A single monsignor in the New York area was asked to handle cases of one ex-priest a month in 1965 and 1966. One had gone to Latin America as a missionary, had been appalled at the need for economic development and had gone back to labor there in that "practical" way. The Peace Corps struck others as a concrete way to help mankind. Sex was a factor in other cases.

Should the Catholic Church reconsider a ban which denies the Latin rite priesthood to married men, and withholds matrimony from the vast share of its clergy (with rare exceptions such as in cases of converted Protestant ministers, or for priests of the Oriental rites of Catholicism)?

Pope Paul VI told the ecumenical council in its final months that he did not want priestly celibacy discussed on the council floor, but he did say that he would study written proposals any bishop cared to make to him. As a result of the initiative of Henri Fesquet, correspondent for *Le Monde,* of Paris, we know of one speech which had been prepared for the council, had the pope not intervened. It was written by Dutch-born Bishop Pierre Koop, of Kins, Brazil. He planned to ask that national conferences of bishops be allowed, with papal consent, to ordain "mature" married men who had been wed "at least five years." The bishop insisted in his prepared text that there was no other way to meet the shortage of clergy in Brazil. His remarks could have been extended to say that, with the exception of Ireland and Boston, few parts of the world are producing the priestly vocations Catholicism finds necessary.

A flood of literature in the middle sixties made the point that celibacy is a harsh burden for some priests, and that boys are asked at an immature age to determine whether they will be able at thirty to hold to a lifelong renunciation of sex and marriage. A range of alternatives was offered. Some suggested that youths go out into parishes for five years after being ordained as deacons, the next to last step before the priesthood and a grade allowing them to give communion, to preach, to marry and to baptize, but withholding the right to say Mass and to hear confessions. The deacons, working among single men and women and married couples of their own age and older, could decide whether to marry and remain at the arrested deacon level, or whether to give up sex, marriage and the joys of family and to go on to the full ministry.

Still others, such as Bishop Alfred Mendez, of Arecibo, Puerto Rico, suggested attacking the problem by attempting to recuperate fallouts of the seminaries and especially of the final theology years of priestly training, inviting them to serve as married deacons. Bishop Mendez answered a questionnaire which I sent to him by saying that Latin America would need 150,000 priests by 1975, and 200,000 by the end of this century, figures "impossible of attainment." Seventeen out of 20 seminarians in Latin America withdrew before ordination, which meant that Puerto Rico alone with 90 native priests (out of a corps of 450 Catholic clergymen) must have a pool of 500 ex-seminarians, ready to be tapped. It would be "easy" to get 30 married deacons from the 100 ex-seminarians in Puerto Rico who had studied philosophy, the bishop was sure, or even from the 50 who had gone as far as the theology years. A few months training of married men in the over-thirty-five group would send out "deacons of the sacraments, or subdeacons" who could marry, baptize, give communion and bury the dead, while a short additional training would turn some of these men into "deacons of the word, full deacons," able to preach short memorized sermons or to embark on longer inspirational speeches. The bishop, using council authorization, was at work on the project in early 1966.

Rarely from priests themselves was there comment on whether many would prefer marriage. The question had been closed for more than a millennium, so much so that a nervous joke went the rounds of clerical circles in Rome at the time of the council's authorization of married deacons: "I think married deacons are a good idea but, frankly, would you want your sister to marry one?"

It was from the pen of a seminarian that one of the most revealing comments came. Steven Nett, a high school junior at Del Bufalo Seminary, Liberty, Missouri, wrote this to *The Catholic Reporter* on October 8, 1965:

> . . . I am studying to become a Precious Blood priest. I have just returned to Del Bufalo after spending three months in my native environment.
>
> The various mundane allurements continue to endanger my vocation. Attraction to girls proved to be the strongest deterrent to my returning. . . . It seemed that it would be so much easier for me to give all my life and all my love to one person here on earth than to continue along that often lonesome path to celibacy. . . .
>
> Before returning to Del Bufalo I had to decide whether my love (for God and mankind) was big enough to answer the staggering

challenge demanded by my vocation. . . . Before returning to Del Bufalo, I . . . had to decide whether I still had, or whether I ever had, the *kind* of love necessary for the priesthood. . . .

The youth went back while many others in his seminary generation dropped out. He said that his bond to his family and the ties he already felt to his order were the deciding factors, but his struggle as he accepted the celibacy sacrifice, the traditional honored mark of full Church service in Latin Catholicism, was evident.

In general, attitudes toward the problem of marriage and the Catholic priesthood were gingerly rooted in the view that it was pointless to discuss something which would not change for generations, if ever. But there were exceptions. *The National Catholic Reporter* of August 4, 1965, provided one. In its characteristically brash way, it said:

We think modification of the discipline on celibacy is advisable. This is, however, a properly tentative conclusion. We are not so tentative, however, about the need for study and discussion. Finally, there are hard-nosed types who say that the authorities in the Church will not take another look at celibacy until or unless forced to it by the pastoral necessity of filling empty pastorates.

Father David P. O'Neill in his *Priestly Celibacy and Maturity*[1] went further. He insisted that the human and Christian values of the wedded state tended to be overlooked by a celibate clergy. He plumped for a parish trial period for deacons who might decide to marry and, beyond that, proposed that the "small minority" of priests who would like to wed should be allowed to do so. They should stay on as priests and would be, he wagered, "as acceptable and useful in the life of the Church as the deacons and celibate priests."

If, indeed, marriage attracted few priests, other factors of change were at work. For one thing, the day of the oracle priest, of the Father Charles E. Coughlin of the thirties who told rapt radio audiences of Catholics about gold problems and money manipulators, was over. Bishop Primeau of New Hampshire noticed the evolution inside his own family. His father had had only six years of grade schooling. He lived in awe of his four priest brothers who were in his view marvelously educated men. The bishop's own brothers were all college graduates. The prelate noticed that they felt on a far more casual footing with him. One function of the priest, to be a guide in all things, was gone.

If the challenge to be a leader in all fields was disappearing, the desire to judge and act in the moral, social and administrative areas of the priest's more specific competence was, if anything, strengthened and often frustrated. The older men who were bishops and pastors were prudent, anxious to preserve and perpetuate what struggling generations had created. There was a diffident, don't-rock-the-boat mentality. Father George H. Dunne spoke of it at the 1963 biennial convention of the National Council of Catholic Men in Atlantic City:

> For too long a distorted version of authoritarianism has reduced the wonted freedom of the children of God to a myth. Clergy, even more than the laity, and perhaps nowhere more than in this country, have been rendered impotent by fear: afraid to act, afraid to write, afraid to speak, afraid even to think. . . . I remember being refused authorization to appear on a platform with the late Marshall Field to discuss the moral basis of post-war rehabilitation, for no other reason than that some Protestant ministers and Jewish rabbis were to be present in the audience, not participating mind you, but merely present. This experience . . . I think, illustrates the prevailing atmosphere in the Church in this country. The paralysis of initiative and mortification of thought which results from this kind of thing is frustrating, stultifying and, in the end, fatal.[2]

On the lowest rung of the clerical ladder curates waiting a quarter of a century for pastorates watched the idiosyncrasies of their all-powerful rectors with a sometimes humorous, sometimes despairing attention. A young priest in one Long Island parish in 1965 crossed up his pastor's efforts to get contributions for the bishop's $24 million high school construction drive by blurting in a Sunday sermon in the church annex: "I think you people pay plenty already. What you should start giving now is yourselves—your minds, your hearts, your civic and social energies." The curate was transferred a few months later with no explanation.

When Pope Paul VI visited the United States in 1965 clergymen thought of one Bronx pastor who seemed to believe that the world existed to flesh out his annual parish parade. On the day of one of these processions, superiors at the diocesan seminary at Dunwoodie, New York, noticed that their seminarian flock of sheep (an apt pastoral symbol), had vanished. In response to the Bronx pastor's "request," they were in the Bronx aboard one of his parade floats. No credit was given to the unwitting Dunwoodie loan.

"I'll bet he'll work the pope into his parade," a monsignor acquaintance commented.

Archbishop Dearden's enlightened Detroit archdiocese did a 1966 survey which reported that "there seems to be no question" but that "in many rectories" the woman housekeeper ranked just below the pastor and well above the young curates, a situation precisely paralleling that in the Vatican during the late years of Pius XII when Mother Pasqualina, chief cook and house cleaner for the pope, was known to be more influential in arranging papal audiences than most of the monsignori and bishops of the Eternal City.

A country bishop, Peter William Bartholome of St. Cloud, Minnesota, once recommended to Cardinal Spellman a way to cope with the New York archdiocesan situation where there was no pastor under the age of forty-eight: "My curates get their own parishes within eight years," said the Minnesotan. "What you should do is to rent space for a chapel every time a new block-square development is under construction. Make the one block a parish in itself and put a young priest in there. He'll get to know all his people that way."

The Minnesotan's reasoning was simple. Ninety-five percent of his Catholics heard Mass, but some city parishes scored an ominously low 30 percent. The thought of turning a back on a tradition of scattered, large, imposing churches was too much for the New York prelate. He did not reply to Bishop Bartholome's free advice.

Even so, some members of the American Catholic community such as Dr. George Shuster, assistant to the president of Notre Dame University, and for twenty years the only Catholic president of a non-Catholic American college (Hunter in New York), were convinced that the small church and the intimate congregation with the priest knowing and involving everyone would be the way of tomorrow.

Are a compulsory retirement age and decent pension plans for pastors and bishops the solution? Should bishops be elected by the clergy and the laity, perhaps limiting ballots to those who are more experienced and active, and possibly giving the pope a choice of three candidates? Should a bishop be limited to an eight-year term, say, in any one diocese, but be eligible for election by the priests and people of another see who might hear of his achievements? Should the election of the pope himself be taken out of the hands of the cardinals and given to a synod of bishops of the world meeting in Rome? Would this give elections to the papacy a less Italian and more universal flavor and, on the national level, would bishops tend less to be self-reproducing, "safe" bureaucratic types, rather than scholars and reformers sensitive to the needs of a rapidly evolving country and world? All of these questions were being raised in quiet conversations among priests and in the pages of the American Catholic press. All reflected a ferment which was bound to alter life in the parishes, in the schoolrooms where Catholics were in attendance, inside the organizations of American Catholics and, most important, the clerical and lay contribution to America.

Part III

Tomorrow's Catholic Americans

EIGHT

A Voice
from the Pew

Two Madison Avenue advertising men, both Catholics, talked one day in the middle sixties about the effects of Pope John's "open window" policy inside their parish churches. One came from the Sands Point area of Nassau County on Long Island, the community F. Scott Fitzgerald satirized as "West Egg," home of the rich, in *The Great Gatsby*.

"Is there anything new in your parish?" the "West Egg" man asked.

"Yes," the suburbanite answered after an instant's thought. "They don't insult us in the sermons any more!"

Further up the "Great Gatsby" peninsula, residents of some other parishes could not say the same. An occasional sermon would denounce "intellectuals in the Church" who predicted changes flowing from Vatican Council II. "The Church is today what it has always been and there will be no change in any essential," curates would thunder.

As English crept into the Mass and suggestions came from the diocese that Masses might be recited facing the people, some reforms were introduced, but pastors and assistants seemed bewildered. One "West Egg" curate perspired as he announced on the Sunday before Lent in 1966 that most of the old fasting had been eliminated by Pope Paul VI. He read the announcement and then waved the paper in the air. "Keep this in mind," he cried. "It will be harder than ever. There won't be simple rules to obey. And remember this too: you can't put any papal document in your coffin as a passport to heaven!"

The crowded congregation sat patiently, accepting one more scolding. The people in the pews seemed only half aware that the lecture appeared to have two targets this time: the laity as usual but, in addition, the pope as well, for making the fasting changes.

The slow evolution on the "West Egg" peninsula away from "insults" reflected significant changes in American Catholic parishes flowing from two causes. On the one hand, there was the stirring among the laity caused by upheavals in other corners of the Church: inside Vatican II, inside the ranks of Bible scholars, within the convents, in the seminaries, and in the rectories. On the other, despite the inescapable reaction, there was the simple end of an era. Even without brave Pope John and historic Vatican II, four centuries of repression symbolized by the Vatican's Index of Forbidden Books, and a century of acclimatization of a once-immigrant American Catholic Church, had concluded with a literate man in the American Catholic pew and a tired, overworked priest in the pulpit. A new relationship was inevitable.

The reaction took many forms. Some clergy and laity found it too hard to change. Some were shocked. What after all was "essential" and "nonessential" in the inheritance? Wasn't nearly everything sacred and untouchable?

In one "West Egg" parish a priest during Pius XII's pontificate, early in the wave of changes, explained that it was no longer necessary to fast from midnight before receiving Holy Communion.

"The pope says so," a curate commented.

An elderly woman parishioner was stunned. "I'll tell you one thing," she informed the priest. "I'm not going to eat at nine A.M. if I'm receiving at ten! If the pope wants to, he can go to Hell, but I won't."

The lesson she had learned as a child was nothing she intended to surrender in advanced age.

Reader Gerald B. McDonald, of New York, used the letters to the editor section of *America* on January 2, 1965, to pour out indignation at wholesale upheavals. He mocked:

This is a go, go, go world. Let's be really modern, 100 percent Americans.

Welcome the transients to our togetherness temples with the *sincere* handshake! A selective group of parish influentials possibly could be prevailed upon to serve as vestibule greeters at each Mass. Neighborhood florists probably would donate tasteful calendar wall posters (with meat and fish days noted), with enthusiasm-building slogans such as: "This is your Bower of Babble. . . . Make yourself heard!" and *"Bray* together and *stay* together." . . . Leave us all get on the ball and make the old church alive in '65!

Threaded between the lines was a complaint of most arch-conservatives: "We are surrendering to a 'Protestantizing' of our religion."

An anonymous contributor to Managing Editor Patrick F. Scanlan's column in *The Tablet* of Brooklyn made a similar point at the same period. He wrote:

I strongly resent being told that the things we were taught all our lives are just old hat, that we never knew what the Mass was all about (because it was in incomprehensible Latin) . . . that we stand to receive the Holy Eucharist (now) because kneeling is a subservient act and as "people of God" we have such great dignity all of a sudden that we no longer have to humble ourselves in receiving Him. We still kneel to the bishops though, I notice!

If all these things are now true, how come we have been so badly taught since the Council of Trent? It certainly seems a sad commentary on our hierarchy, priests and the "intelligentsia" that at a time when they are knocking themselves out to please the Protestants—removing statues of the Blessed Virgin from her altar . . . , hosting and attending innumerable conferences on how to "live significantly" with Jews, Protestants, atheists and so forth— they have apparently neither the time nor the inclination to be even civil or concerned about the faithful parishioners who are begging simply for a chance to worship in a way that is meaningful to them. All we hear is forget it!

Those reacting were by no means only laymen. The St. Paul *Catholic Bulletin* in late 1965 carried a sermon of Monsignor Rudolph G. Bandas: "You know as well as I do that when you open windows (Pope John's expression) you may admit foul as well as fresh air, and if you open them too wide some queer birds may enter and cause chaos and confusion within."

Fifty-nine-year-old Bishop Leo Smith faced expressions of dismay one day in 1964 when he outlined plans for introducing English into the Mass. Before him sat priests of a northern New York State diocese.

"I'm eighty," one cleric said. "I'm too old. Can't those like me just ignore this for the little while we have left?"

"No," Bishop Smith answered. "Pope John was eighty and he changed. All of us must too."

The essential transition facing the American Catholic parish in the middle sixties was the need to reduce the almost total powers vested in the hands of pastors. Authority had to be shared out among curates and nuns inside the first parish circle, and then among the laity through parish finance committees, school boards and other control groups reaching into each phase of parish life. For many pastors and even for a large number of curates this was unthinkable. Among laymen a mixed reaction was evident: a desire to enter more deeply into the practice of their religion, and a reluctance or even an inability to subtract much time from the support of their families and their roles as citizens active inside their religiously plural communities.

Making it especially hard for many pastors was the memory of earlier decades when pious laymen sought the priest's leadership on everything including local elections, if the clergyman was indiscreet enough to drop hints in that regard. In many parishes, especially in Boston and New York, the attitude was a throwback to other centuries in Ireland when the French-educated priest was often the only member of the flock who had had any sort of formal education.

The America of the final third of the twentieth century was another world with parishes in the large cities crowded with holders of advanced academic degrees and board members of large corporations, but old relationships die slowly. In mid-century the bishop of Sinclair Lewis' "Babbitt" country north of St. Paul (Bishop Peter William Bartholome of Saint Cloud) was still telling his priests: "Remember in all your sermons and in all you do, keep the simple lay folk in mind."

Father Yzermans, who became a monsignor and spokesman of the American hierarchy in Washington, was one of the young clerics who listened, unconvinced, to such counsels. He and some of his colleagues did a study to determine just how "simple" the people of the heavily Catholic "Main Street" area were. They came up with the startling information that 40 percent of the farmers were college graduates.

Even so, a few old-timers in the pews helped preserve the illusion of an untaught laity. One such, an old German woman, praised Father Yzermans one day as he completed a sermon.

"Father," she said, "you talk so good—out of your head!"

Her seraphic expression made clear that she had no intention of implying that he was "out of" his mind.

A slip of the tongue reflecting the old intellectually superior attitude of the clergy was caught by the watchful Dan

Herr and published in his satiric column in *The Critic* in December, 1965. It was a portion of a statement made by Monsignor George Shea of Darlington, New Jersey, at a Vatican Council press panel. The monsignor had said: "The Church has a duty to its own members, and should assure some of our *simple-minded* faithful . . ."

By no means all of the laity of the twentieth century's final years were simple-minded or even simple, but respect for followers and the delegation of authority are arts not every leader learns. In many parishes, in the words of Monsignor Yzermans, the pastor was still "the old Irishman who tells the housekeeper when the rectory needs new towels, and instructs the gardener when the grass needs mowing."

Far from making use of the talents flourishing in the pews of the 1960s, many a pastor ran his parish school and church without a word of advice from anyone, and disdained kid gloves as he dealt with parishioners.

For that, too, the candid, amiable Monsignor Yzermans had a story: "In my home area [the Sinclair Lewis country] we had one old pastor who was sure, and probably with good reason, that everyone listened in on the party line when he got a call at the rectory. Every night just before turning in to sleep he would ring his own number and say: 'Good night, dear people, I'm going to bed now.' Another pastor used to bawl out the operator when she would ask him the number he wanted. 'I know whom I'm calling, it's your job to know the number,' he'd say."

This was what Monsignor Yzermans labeled "clerical brusqueness." In an open house for the press at the Manchester, New Hampshire, diocese in 1965, the hierarchy spokesman told 100 New England newspapermen gathered at the diocesan chancery that he wished to use the occasion to apologize to newsmen everywhere for all the times in which they had been victims of rough ecclesiastical handling.

This reporter was able to reach back thirty years into his

own memories to recall one occasion of not merely clerical but even episcopal "brusqueness" which seemed to fit within the limits of the monsignor's definition. I had gone to a Brooklyn rectory to inquire about some parish embarrassment brought on by human nature's many weaknesses. The pastor, an open, gentle person, was willing to reveal the truth, although he was not happy about advertising the trouble. He asked me to wait while he placed one telephone call. He explained the situation into the mouthpiece and then blushed as he got his instructions.

"That was the bishop," he said. "He told me to throw you out!"

The vigilant *Catholic Reporter* spotted one remarkable example of "clerical brusqueness" which it published on January 7, 1966, in "Cry Pax, a column without rules!"

From the December 19 (1965) bulletin of the Church of the Holy Cross, Minneapolis:
"CONFESSIONS. Do not wait with confessions until the last minute. Come early. Do not call the rectory for time of Mass or confessions. Only very indifferent Catholics would do that. If you can't remember the time of confessions, well, stay away. It will do no good for you anyway."

The tireless Dan Herr had one more contribution to the list.

From a news story. "A Catholic priest in the tree-lined borough of Fairview, N.J., has suspended two members of his parish from any activities because he says they insulted him at a recent meeting of the town's board of education.

"One of the men suspended, Emmanuel Triggiano, is president of the school board. The other, Ciro Scarpulla, is a board member. . . .

"Suspension for Triggiano means he can no longer serve as an usher at Masses nor take part in the activities of the Holy Name Society. Scarpulla loses his position as a leader of the church's Boy

Scout troop, his membership in the Holy Name Society and his usher's job."[1]

The problem of how the pastor should deal with the evolving layman drew the attention of at least one bishop, Ernest L. Unterkoefler, of Charleston, South Carolina. He told participants at the 1965 National Liturgical Week conference: "The lack of courtesy and moderation is, alas, one of the most frequent and pernicious causes for estrangement of the faithful from their pastors; it also shows little understanding of the effects of modern education which no longer tolerates abuses of authority, rough treatment, disrespect or bad manners."

If the better educated, more affluent laity of the latter 1900s were restless under pastors' heavy hands, there was nonetheless the corollary of the parish priest who struggled vainly to comprehend the strange new man seated before him in the pews. We are indebted to "Cry Pax" again for an item from the parish bulletin of St. Jeremiah's Church, Framingham, Massachusetts. Written no doubt after a meeting of minds inside a rectory sitting room, the bulletin notice plugged a tea to be given by the Sodality of Our Lady. It said, and the hand of the earnest rector could be seen forming the words: "To help attendance, the pastor assures you he will not attend."[2]

Sociological studies, something new inside Catholicism, repeatedly reported a lay-clerical tension in the parishes. A public relations man for a great airline told how this resolved itself in his parish inside a New Jersey town which prides itself as the birthplace of one of the astronauts.

"Our pastor is seventy-four," the public relations man said. "He is real Irish. He has done a great deal for us. He put up a good high school. But the sermons ramble now. And we worry about the grade school. They can't get the right teachers for it. Fifteen years ago, before I moved into the town, two or three hundred in the parish sent a petition to the bishop, saying that they appreciated all that had been done, especially the building of the high school, but they wished respectfully to request the assignment of a new pastor."

The bishop, as often happens in such cases, sent the petition back to the rector. The latter preached about it at the Masses on the following Sunday, commenting bitterly on what he interpreted as ingratitude. No changes were made.

"Now," said the advertising man, "many go to other parishes nearby. The pastor won't let any of the curates come to the meetings of our Holy Name Society (parish men's organization). The Holy Name really comes down to four corporate Communions a year, and nothing else. Many men of talent are in the parish and would like to lend their services, but they are never asked.

"And yet the pastor prides himself on being a widely-read man. This new best-seller *In Cold Blood* by Truman Capote, the pastor will read it. I'm sure of that."

A reverse solution to the typical parish crisis occurred in 1956 at St. Francis de Sales Church, in Holland, Michigan, and may prove to be the answer.

Parishioner John F. Donnelly, a business executive, spoke in 1965 as president of the National Council of Catholic Men and told what had happened at St. Francis. The pastor, he said, was "a good man—meticulous, reliable, there when needed and overworked; overworked . . . by his own choice, for he consistently refused any proffered help."

St. Francis, said the president of the Catholic laymen of the United States, was "a good parish, fairly bursting to do something," but "of lay activity there was almost none." The pastor "did not forbid all lay activity but he created so chill an atmosphere it did not flourish."

The old rector died and the bishop attended his funeral. Laymen of St. Francis begged the prelate for a modern,

131

cooperative leader, and named the man they preferred, Monsignor Arthur LeRoux, a pioneer in giving laymen a role in liturgical services. The bishop said nothing, but Monsignor LeRoux arrived as new rector. A financial crisis faced him at once. The former pastor had spent $180,000 on a convent for merely four nuns; the parish school was in a dismal state. Two laymen were helping the four nuns teach a student body of 350. The lay salaries were only three fifths of what the nearby public school was paying. The monsignor set up the first of a series of parish lay-clerical committees to go over each of the problems. One of the first discoveries was that the geography teacher, a sister, was using 1932 textbooks a dozen years after World War II had scrambled the map of Europe and of much of Africa and Asia. Sister explained why she had never notified the principal, let alone the pastor: "I thought the parish was too poor to get new ones."

The lay-clerical board with the future president of the NCCM as a central force raised teacher salaries to just under the public school level, got up-to-date geography books, and found an insurer who was willing to give health and accident coverage to the parish's small staff of lay employes. So far as John Donnelly was able to learn, St. Francis de Sales was the country's first joint lay-clerical school board, but bishop after bishop since then has instructed pastors to set up similar forums for the tapping of the professional experience and human wisdom of congregations. Scores of parishes followed the Holland, Michigan, lead although Mrs. Katherine B. O'Neill, speaking at the 1963 NCCM convention in Atlantic City, still had to report that the 11,000 parochial schools and 2,500 Catholic high schools of the country had only 4,000 parent-teacher organizations among all of them. Lay and parental involvement in the schools and in the central parish decisions was on the way, but it was still surprisingly laggardly in coming.

What greater contribution could laymen make in their

parishes? What more did they wish to do? Some doubted that laymen really wanted to do much more than "believe, pray, pay, and obey," as Bishop Ernest Primeau, of New Hampshire, phrased it at the ecumenical council.

"The problem," said Monsignor O'Neil C. D'Amour, diocesan superintendent of schools in Marquette, Michigan, "is not primarily that of a clergy defending entrenched privilege, it is that of a laity loath to assume responsibilities. The picture of a laity ready and anxious to assume responsibilities is not . . . true. . . . [There are] some such . . . but they are relatively few." Most priests, said the monsignor, find that "the emerging laymen quickly submerge when offered responsibility coupled with work."[3]

Even so, the monsignor added, the best guess was that, by 1970, lay-clerical boards of education would be governing 90 percent of American Catholic parochial schools, something which not one parish envisioned during the days of the early friction at St. Francis de Sales.

To be able to set up parish school boards inside so much of the American Catholic Church organization within so short a time—less than one and one-half decades—implied some lay willingness to participate more fully. Indeed there were many signs that a substantial share of the laity wished to participate intimately in the life of their Church.

"Many of the pastors thought they'd have to beat the laymen over the head to get some of them into the sanctuary when the liturgical changes came in," Monsignor Yzermans reports, "but the fact is that all that was needed in a large share of the cases was to say 'volunteer lectors are to show up Tuesday,' and more than enough applied."

Father Joseph H. Fichter, a sociologist, reported in *Priest and People*[4] how he sent questionnaires to 4,560 parish priests and to 4,500 laymen, probing their attitudes. The laity characteristically, Father Fichter found, spoke appreciatively of their clergy but repeatedly sounded one theme: a

133

desire for a greater involvement in their parishes and for closer relations with the clergy.

Father Fichter spoke even more clearly in a paper the American hierarchy asked him to do for them in January, 1964.[5] In that report the priest said that five fundamental principles of human relations which "do not seem to be practiced by bishops and clergy in the Catholic Church" had to be put into effect inside each parish if the best results were to be achieved:

Parishioners had to be "trusted."

Those given tasks inside a parish must have sufficient authority and leeway for step-by-step decisions on the way to the accomplishment of the central assignment.

The man who works must get recognition for what he accomplishes.

Each one doing a job must be told how well or poorly he is performing it.

"Open communications" between clergy and laymen should hold parish surprises to a minimum.

In short, the sociologist told the bishops, "American people simply resent paternalism: they do not like to be treated like children."

What Father Fichter was outlining was the necessary parish of the future and by no means the parish or diocese of the middle sixties. When even the enlightened Bishop Primeau, of New Hampshire, a man of the future inside the American national delegation to Vatican II, held his unprecedented open house for the press at his chancery in Manchester in 1965, the chore assigned to the layman who was manager of a chain of local motion picture houses was to serve as chauffeur for the day's visitors.

Stephen McNierney, an editor of *The Book of Catholic Worship,* recalled in the March, 1966, *U.S. Catholic* that a top story in the Catholic press of a few years earlier was the case of the prominent business executive who asked his pastor how he could help. The clergyman pondered and then asked his caller to mow the rectory lawn.

But in the first months of 1966 the same man would be tapped as head of an adult education program or appointed to the parish financial advisory board or "at least would be named a lector," Mr. McNierney said, as a token of change.

A lay contributor to a forum on the laity in the ultra-conservative *The Tablet* of Brooklyn outlined these aspirations on June 24, 1965: "Our responsibilities . . . should involve something a little more agonizing than the annual bazaar and something a little more profound than handling the roll-call at the Holy Name meeting. These responsibilities should include at least the right to suggest the time of Masses and Confessions and topics for the Sunday sermon."

Monsignor Timothy Flynn, pastor of the only church in the Western Hemisphere ever visited by a pope (the Church of the Holy Family, New York's parish center for the United Nations), found that his parishioners were helpful in recommending questions to be included and omitted in a parish census.

"They'd say, 'No, you can't very well ask that, people would resent it,'" the monsignor, who was Cardinal Francis J. Spellman's press spokesman, said. "So I'd leave that out.

"And I have a group of twenty-five-year-old young-marrieds who want to be shock troops, going wherever the parish needs. So I accept that. Then, too, there's the Legion of Mary. About fifteen attend its meetings. They go to hospitals and so forth."

At forty-nine years of age in the middle sixties the white-haired priest was the youngest pastor in Cardinal Spellman's archdiocese, and one of the few active innovators. Old plaster of paris statues of the Virgin and saints vanished from his church and were replaced by such modern substitutes as a chapel honoring Italian aviators "martyred" in the Congo in the early sixties on a United Nations relief mission. The priest even had a modish young woman in her early thirties walk, accompanied by a man, to the railless altar bringing bread and wine for use at the consecration of the Mass. Parishioners were kept busy reading ritual responses to the prayers in English recited by a priest whose back no longer was turned to them.

"Of course," the monsignor shrugged off the objections of reactionaries, "I get cracks like: 'That was very nice, Father; when do I come back to say my prayers?' "

The work of moving an old Church forward into a new world of educated and responsible lay people had been begun in Monsignor Flynn's parish, but most other neighborhood churches groped for a way in which the man in the pew could speak to the clergyman in the pulpit. The NCCM, in its copyrighted 1965 kit on the parish repercussions of Vatican II, suggested that a letters-to-the-editor section might be included in a pastor's weekly bulletin. Many a parish would have long to wait before any such change as that would occur, but pressing for similar innovations was both the letter of the Vatican II decrees assigning new rights and responsibilities to laymen, and also considerations such as those outlined by Father Raymond R. Shevlin, who in early 1966 became the first new moderator of the Brooklyn Holy Name Society in thirty years. He said: "It is mathematically and physically impossible for the parish priests and religious to do the job that is required. They must have the help of the laity in the work of salvation in the parish."

However reluctant the pastor and the parishioner, a more active and dignified role for the layman in the Church's work in each parish was inescapable.

NINE

The Intellectual's Day

In no area of American Catholic life was dramatic change more evident than in the schoolroom and on the college campus. The old arguments about "anti-intellectualism" continued to flare in the letters-to-the-editor columns of Church publications, but hundreds of thousands of graduates of Catholic and of secular colleges and universities promised prompt and vast transformations inside the parishes, within the Catholic educational system and, indeed, in the Catholic influence on America itself.

A rear guard attached to an anti-literate, even anti-cultural, earlier era kept up the battle against revision, evidently unaware that nothing could prevent a massive impact from modern education. An example was the parish priest in the "West Egg" section of Long Island who struggled one morning to make the valid point that a Catholic school diploma, a faddish interest in "intellectual" things, a love for change for its own sake, and a dilettante's attraction to various social "causes" were no substitute for ancient ideals of spirituality.

"Some of the greatest saints have been just plain stupid," the preacher said. "And as for all this talk about social action, well, some of the greatest saints were hermits who didn't do any at all."

The priest spoke from a background which Cardinal Eugene Tisserant had observed in an American tour in the late thirties.

"I saw many of the bishops," the dean of the College of Cardinals told me a quarter of a century later. "What I saw and heard astonished me. I went back to Pius XI and told him, 'The American hierarchy has no intellectual interests!' "

For Tisserant, a man with a command of 15 languages, a community withdrawn from the world of cultural and social interests was unimaginable.

A favorite argument of the anti-intellectuals was that the world has never had so much information at its fingertips, as a result of the proliferation of universities and the explosive advances in the use of computers, yet troubles remain. Sometimes the editors' correspondents used almost the same words to drive home their point. *The Tablet* of the Brooklyn diocese, for instance, ran these letters two months apart:

From Eli Eliezer, of Chicago, August 18, 1964:

COMMON SENSE, NOT EDUCATION.

It would be far better if potential "dropouts" were taught a manual trade rather than stay in high school. Then they could be . . . self-supporting at the age of 18. Education is not the answer to our problems. What we need is wisdom and common sense, but none of our schools can teach that. Public education is the rule. . . . Yet the world is in greater turmoil and chaos than ever before. . . . I do not appeal against education, only to put education in its proper perspective. . . . For too long we have ignored the wisdom of common folks. . . .

And from O. C. Herman, Swannanoa, North Carolina, October 15, 1964:

Bravo to Sarah Clingain for defending the illiterates' right to vote. If it takes an education to vote intelligently, why don't educated people agree on some things? . . . Some are anti-Communist, some are anti-anti-Communist. And some are just plain morons. The world has more schools, books, colleges and libraries than in any time in history and is in the worst condition than ever before. It's too bad colleges can't teach common sense.

An article in *America* at about the same time made the point that unschooled, authoritarian, immigrant family atmospheres had hampered the growth of literary interests among Catholics. It brought an indignant retort from William V. Kennedy, of Washington, who mentioned that he had the military rank of major:

One of my grandfathers, a shipyard craftsman, scraped together, from God only knows where, the money to buy sets of Dickens and Shakespeare, and any other classics he could lay his hands on. He used his "authoritarian" control . . . to insure that his children read these books rather than the trash foisted on them by the society in which they lived. . . . Let us not ignore the fact that the term "intellectual" as used during the past 40 years or so has come to include so odd a lot, including more than a handful of outright traitors, that it is questionable whether the term is not now quite as opprobrious as its opposite.

Major Kennedy added a scornful reference to "imitation Yankees," meaning, presumably, those people who seek to emulate the bookish products of Harvard, Radcliffe, Smith, Yale, Amherst, Williams, Brown and the other old colleges and universities associated with the early New England tradition.

Running through all of the controversy was the idea that virtue, wisdom and love of life's finer values were not necessarily identified with higher education. However true that might be, there was also an implicit hostility toward formal education and a tendency to exalt the lack of it.

A variant form of anti-intellectualism was specific antipathy for the reading of books. What no doubt in history began with profound reverence for The Book, for Holy Scripture, and evolved through recent centuries into an Index-fostered concern about irreligious and immoral volumes, seemed to jell among many Catholics, clergy and laity alike, into an aversion to books themselves. The fundamentalist non-Catholic Jehovah's Witnesses summed up this tendency in a warning at their 1965 convention at Yankee Stadium in New York: "Be careful about any book you pick up. Keep in mind that reading a book is engaging in a conversation with an author, and it is a conversation in which you cannot talk back!"

The antibook cast of mind was the subject of a December 16, 1965, article by James G. Murray in *The Long Island Catholic,* of which he is editor for books. He said that his telephone and his mail brought him a flood of comments from parents obsessed, not with the books which they and their children should read, but rather with those they should ban. Typical comments, he said, were these:

"My teenage daughter has to write a report on X for her junior high school English class. I hear it's a dirty book. Is it?"

"My son, a senior at the local high school, has to read Y for his social studies teacher. The fellow who wrote that book is a Communist, isn't he? Do you think they ought to assign that sort of thing?"

"That book by Z is atheistic, wouldn't you say? My kids shouldn't read it, should they?"

The targets of many of these thrusts were J. D. Salinger's *Catcher in the Rye* ("dirty"), Harper Lee's *To Kill a Mockingbird* ("Lee loves violence"), George Orwell's *1984* ("Orwell is against the American way of life"), and William

140

Golding's *Lord of the Flies* ("Golding is an atheist"). Mr. Murray defended all four as books which "level up, not down." With his forthright presentation in *The Long Island Catholic,* Murray provided one step forward toward a more intimate, literate Catholic participation in American life.

The Index of forbidden books, which began to pass into the discard after Pope John XXIII's Vatican Council II, was unquestionably at the root of some American Catholic attitudes toward the main published works. Tracing to the decades just after the invention of the printing press and the rise of the Protestant Reformation, the Index was a chronic source of embarrassment to Catholic scholarship, even though Cardinal Alfredo Ottaviani, head of the Holy Office (the former Inquisition), told Mrs. Anna Brady, the Rome correspondent of *The Long Island Catholic* (as reported in the April 14, 1966, issue), that no new books had been added since 1947, and that none ever again would be.

The decision, encouraged by the ecumenical council, was not a year too soon in coming, in the opinion of many churchmen for, as Father Harold M. Watson, of St. Benedict's College, Atchison, Kansas, pointed out in *America,* ironies abounded: the works of some authors were condemned while others, little different, went unnoticed. The priest found it objectionable that all of Balzac, Stendhal, Georges Sand, the Dumases, Zola, Gide and Sartre were on the Index, thus depriving Catholics, in the case of Stendhal works, of "meeting some of the greatest characters of literature, like Julien Sorel, Mme. de Renal, Mathilde de la Mole, Fabrice, Mosca, and Sanseverina." Galileo, the father of much modern astronomy, stayed on the Index until 1882, and, Father Watson added as an evidence of the Index's slow correction of earlier errors, *Paradise Lost* and Dante's *De Monarchia* until 1900. Finally, even more startling, he commented, a typographical error in Father Redmond Burke's *What Is the Index?* (the omission of a line saying "Works which may be read by all") caused many Catholic librarians to lock up 148 "permissible love stories," mostly by the elder Dumas, Balzac and Sand. Included in the 148 were *The Three Musketeers* and its sequel, *Twenty Years After*. The librarians thought mistakenly that this list, too, fell under the Index ban.

The result of all the anti-literate influences was indicated in a survey in the early sixties by Notre Dame University's *Ave Maria* magazine. Questionnaires were sent to 24,000 graduates of Catholic colleges, asking what books they read. Twenty percent replied—a group large enough to permit generalizations. Thirty-two percent never read books. Men were the greater offenders. Forty-four percent of them never wandered beyond newspapers, magazines and the television set. Of those who read books, only 21 percent looked at "Catholic" titles. "Spiritual reading," on the one hand, and, on the other, general titles of the best-seller variety had some following. There was almost no audience for tomes dealing with the philosophical and sociological problems facing a Catholic in secularist and pluralist modern America.

The evidences of lag were in every parish pew; yet in the middle sixties, the American Catholic layman was moving swiftly into a new era in which his rapidly expanding culture and education would affect the whole of the Catholic parochial and diocesan high school system and the Church and American society as well. Changes were coming partly because of a sudden abandonment of a tradition of all-clerical control of the Church's kindergarten-to-graduate-school educational system. Pastors invited laymen onto parish school boards. Parent-teacher organizations were set up for the first time. Laymen were taken onto diocesan school boards. Others of the laity were chosen as vice-presidents and even as presidents of Church colleges and universities. Perhaps more importantly, the nuns, brothers and priests who once monopolized the faculties of the greater share of the schools were joined by an army of laymen.

Between 1950 and 1964 the number of laymen teaching in the 14,315 Catholic elementary and high schools, colleges and universities quadrupled, reaching a total of 80,580—40 percent of the faculties of the schools. In such institutions as St. John's University, Brooklyn, five sixths of the 600 faculty members were laymen. In St. John's case, at the start of the sixties only 10 percent of the faculty were members of the Vincentian order which held all but one of the dozen seats on the board of trustees. That, incidentally, set up tensions which caused the first teacher strike in American university history.

The influx of laymen was caused by a shortage of vocations. In its turn it forced a severe inflation of school budgets. Nuns often had starved for the honor of starting small colleges. Lay instructors with families could not help but ask for salaries at least approximating those in other colleges. A study done in the 1963–64 school year by the American Association of University Professors showed that the average nine-month salary in church-related universities, very many of them Catholic, was only $8,652, compared with $9,367 in public universities and $10,886 in independent private institutions. The gap was closing, however, due in part to the increasing authority being turned over to laymen inside the governing boards and the administrations of the Catholic universities. This was a trend which was likely to accelerate for, as Martin Work, executive director of the National Council of Catholic Men, commented in *Our Sunday Visitor,* on January 2, 1966, broad new sums were needed for the Catholic educational system and could not be expected unless laymen who provided them had a voice in the spending. Mr. Work said: "Our educational institutions at every level need vast injections of funds if they are to provide high quality instruction. The necessary money will only be forthcoming if the laity have something to say about how these institutions are conducted and how the money is spent. Co-responsibility is a two-way street."

As one of the handful of American lay auditors at Vatican II, the tall, gangly Mr. Work was uniquely placed to comment on this central question of American Catholic education.

The immensity of the American Catholic sacrifice in behalf of a religiously centered education is hard to comprehend, especially when it is considered that it has been financed by poorer strata of the population over the course of the past century and at the same time as regular tax payments were made toward the parallel public school system. On April 17, 1963, John F. Donnelly, president of the National Council of Catholic Men, said that "a good estimate of the cost of Catholic education" was "upwards of $2 billion." He compared that with the total budget of the United Fund ($520 million) and the combined local and national disbursements of the Red Cross ($89 million). The National Catholic Educational Association in a booklet, *The Human Purpose of Catholic Education,* cited an even higher cost estimate in 1965. Based on the $532 it takes each year to care for a student in public elementary and high schools, the Catholic saving to the country could be calculated at $3,231,-073,804 a year, the NCEA said.

By whatever reckoning, the cost has been huge, and leaders both in the hierarchy and in the laity have been appraising the results with some unhappiness. For parents who wish their children to compete successfully for the highest and most influential positions in American society, results often have been poor.

Catholic education aspires to every level of instruction, including the doctorate, but Michael Novak, a sharp-penned student of the American Catholic scene, pointed out in *Commonweal* on January 25, 1963, that Cornell University alone gave more doctoral degrees in the decade ending in 1958 than all 320 American Catholic colleges and universities combined. The Catholic Church school system boasted of

12.5 percent of the country's enrollment, but the Novak study showed that only 2,354 out of 83,439 doctorates given nationally came from Catholic campuses.

The emphasis on research, which is a mark of a college's intellectual vitality, is notably low on Catholic campuses, as Father Donald Zewe, a Jesuit, pointed out in a review of John D. Donovan's *The Academic Man in the Catholic College*.[1] Studies, as Father Zewe underlined, showed 46 percent of Catholic college faculty members listing themselves primarily as teachers and only 2 percent describing themselves as researchers first. Father Zewe speculated, on the basis of the Donovan text, that the mother's strong role and the Catholic family's insistence on obedience and dependence as principal childhood virtues might be at the root of this.

Whatever the cause, the signs of inferior scholarly accomplishment were everywhere. As early as January, 1958, *The Catholic World* pointed out that "the limitations of Catholic schools are revealed each time the National Science Foundation fellowships are distributed; in 1956 the foundation gave out 775 fellowships. Only 17 went to students in Catholic colleges." The following year's results confirmed the observation; of 1,845 fellowships bestowed, the Catholic college share was 19.

In whatever field of community activity, the shortcomings of the world's largest private school system were reflected. The Right Reverend Monsignor George G. Higgins, director of the social action department of the National Catholic Welfare Conference, asked in the Marquette University lecture series (March 28, 1962), "Christian Thought in the Modern World," whether American Catholics were "pulling their weight in the field of scholarship and higher learning." His answer was an anguished no. Catholics, with their background of the papal social encyclicals and their prominence in the history of the American labor movement, ought to be eminent at least in the area of industrial research, but, he said, a contemporary study published by the Industrial Relations Research Association gave the lie to that. The book, *Decade of Industrial Relations Research: 1946–1956*,[2] listed 300 to 400 volumes, monographs and scholarly articles, with only "a tiny handful by Catholic scholars or [written] under the auspices of Catholic institutions of higher learning."

It was not even possible to say that the reason for the failure was because of a scholarly concentration on things of the spirit. Monsignor John Tracy Ellis, the historian, of the University of San Francisco, pointed out in a letter to *America* on March 6, 1965, that "Concilium," which he described as "a very ambitious and promising venture in international Catholic scholarship," had found only 13 Americans worthy, in the organizers' opinion, to qualify for the editorial staff of about 250. Almost all the rest were Europeans. "Concilium" was a set of books to be published between 1965 and 1970 setting forth Catholicism's message to the world in ten main areas. For one of the ten an American general editor was chosen, Father Roland E. Murphy, editor of *The Catholic Biblical Quarterly*. That was in the field of Scriptural studies. In five areas—Dogma, Pastoral Theology, Moral Theology, the Church and the World, and Spirituality—no Americans were tapped. The American showing in the other five fields: Scriptures, 4 out of 21; Ecumenism, 5 out of 27; Liturgy, 2 of 27; Canon Law, 1 in 12; and Church History, 1 in 17.

A serious divorce from the world can be traced back to some parochial schools. Dr. Paul Mundy of Loyola University, Chicago, polled thirty-eight Catholic grade school principals and found these results:[3]

Fifty-four percent were unable to give the names of their two United States senators.
Eighty-six percent did not know their congressman's name.

Seventy-eight percent said that none of the sisters on their staffs took part in activities of an adult organization.

Eighty percent of the principals were acquainted with no local non-Catholic clergyman.

Seventy-six percent had never attended a meeting of any community organization.

Forty-six percent could not cite the name of any local civic group.

With so many inherited handicaps it would seem impossible for the American Catholic layman ever to shoulder the social tasks which the fathers of Vatican II urged upon him. Yet curiously, for good or ill, that role in United States life was approaching rapidly for the 50 million American Catholic laymen precisely because of higher education, although not because of Catholic education. The "non-Catholic" college by the middle sixties was training two thirds of the American Catholics receiving a higher education, and by 1985, according to Philadelphia's archbishop, John J. Kroll, the proportion of those in the so-called secular institutions would be over 80 percent.[4]

Leadership is the prerogative of the educated man. It was evident in the middle sixties that the men and women who would rise as guides for their fellow American Catholic laity in the final two decades of this century would be secular, not Catholic, graduates. Their emphasis would be on scholarship and democracy, not on tired authoritarian ways of a century and a half earlier.

Priests, nuns and laymen at the peak of Catholic education were among the first to recognize this immense change wrought both by financial shortages on the Catholic campuses and by a general demand for better academic accomplishments. Sister Margaret, the president of Trinity College in Washington, D.C., warned at a one-day symposium in Purchase, New York, in 1965, that the day of the Catholic girls' weak little college with a student body of 500 was coming to an end. "The mediocre, the follow-the-leaders, the watchers-of-the-woods will fade," she predicted.

In its place, an army of Catholic educators predicted, would come consolidations of small Catholic institutions, and tie-ins between Catholic and secular educational centers at every level of the instructional process (with Catholic high schools built cheek by jowl with public institutions so that the Catholic students could take courses at taxpayers' expense at the next-door institutions, and with Catholic colleges set up at the edge of great universities and tied in with them for some studies as in Toronto, Canada). Even more than that, the Catholic share of higher education would shrink proportionately as federal funds gushed into public campuses. Richard J. Clifford and William R. Callahan, two Jesuit theology students at Weston College, Weston, Massachusetts, members of an order which has long dominated American Catholic higher education, predicted that the 1960 statistics of one American student in twelve on a Catholic campus would be reduced by 1985 to one in twenty-five.[5]

Not all American Catholic educators lamented this trend away from the small Catholic day-hop college to the large campus and the progressively greater influence of the secular institutions. Dr. George Shuster, who for twenty years was the only Catholic serving as president of an American secular college (New York City's Hunter College for women), told students at St. Meinrad's Seminary in the early sixties that "secular" was a bad word for the average non-Catholic college. He preferred "uncommitted" for, he said, Catholic teachers and scholars are "cordially welcomed and dealt with on a basis of complete equality." The touchstone was academic competence, he said, adding: "The vast majority of Catholics now belong to social strata which properly deem intellectual training an absolute essential."

The future, said Dr. Shuster, a former assistant to the

148

president of Notre Dame University, "will be colored by the extent to which religion permeates learning and, conversely, how learning permeates religion. . . . A rapidly increasing number of young people will not be served by Catholic educational institutions. . . . We shall have to deal, on its own terms and not ours, with . . . secular education."

Other Catholic leaders showed the same equanimity as they watched the trend toward "non-Catholic" education. Andrew P. Moloney, a New York banker, president of the board of trustees of the foundation set up by the American Catholic bishops for the Newman "apostolate" to the "uncommitted" campus, said at a Golden Jubilee celebration of the Newman movement on August 31, 1965:

Above all . . . Catholic lay leaders must be sought out on the *secular campus*. Emphasis must be placed here for both quantitative and qualitative reasons, quantitative . . . [because] at present two out of every three Catholics receive their higher education on a secular campus . . . [and] qualitative also . . . for on the secular campus the quality of Catholic lay leadership is among the finest. The picture is bright. This leadership is manifested in an ambition, initiative, drive and tenacity that is surpassed only by its theological underpinnings. . . .

The graduates of the Newman movement, in the view of Bishop Primeau, of New Hampshire, were battlers who had learned to struggle to reconcile their Church and scholarship and who would surely be heard from as men who would by no means be mute in their local church vestibules.

With the help of gifts of $10,000 to $20,000 each solicited quietly from a few laymen in the main dioceses, Mr. Moloney's foundation was setting about a herculean task in the middle sixties. Aware that there were more Catholics at Purdue than at Notre Dame, and more at New York University than at the Jesuits' Fordham, the foundation was attempting to finance an apostolate of priests, nuns, brothers and laymen to bring Catholic devotion and philosophy to the secular campuses. Where possible, courses in religion were offered for local college or university credit. At least a friendly priest or two would be available part time to plead the case of ancient moral codes before a scientific, inquiring generation which had placed almost all the old inheritances in the test tube for reexamination. In the minds of some of the Newman leaders the real target was not the Catholic student but his frequently dereligionized non-Catholic classmate. Father Robert E. Kavanaugh, chaplain of the students' parish at Michigan State University, pointed out, for instance,[6] that 66 percent of all churchgoers at the state school were Catholics. The church-attending Roman Catholics were only 20 percent of the student body. Michigan State's real problem, said the chaplain, was "the actual tragic loss of faith among the Protestant students." Seventy percent of the student body, he underlined, attended the services of no church.

Would the Catholic Church get very far in "baptizing" America's secular universities? The answer to that was no, but it was nonetheless true that the "apostolate" to the secular campus was becoming a major project of the American Catholic Church. In 1893 when the first club in the name of the erudite Anglican convert, Cardinal John Henry Newman, was founded by five students and one priest at the University of Pennsylvania, the immigrant American Catholic Church commonly shunned United States secular higher education as beyond the pale. The Church felt unwanted on the campuses of the nonsectarian scholars and made no effort to converse.

By 1965, 1,022 priests and a pioneer band of 12 nuns were in the Newman apostolate. Only 250 of the clergy were assigned full time to the student work. Nine hundred and sixty-eight secular campuses had some sort of Newman activity, but only 203 had centers of their own, and of these, only 90 were considered by the national leadership as "reasonably adequate."

A measure of the problem was given by Mr. Clifford and Mr. Callahan, the Jesuit theology students, in their September, 1964, *America* article. In 1954, they said, the American Catholic community had one priest for 660 laymen. By 1965 the vocation shortage had changed the proportions to one priest for 785 of the laity. If the Newman clergy were to maintain the ordinary parish proportions, 915 would be needed on secular campuses, instead of merely 250 full-time clerics. That, of course, would be without any apostolate to what Father Kavanaugh described as the "seventy percent of our graduates, our future [national] leaders [who] are sincere agnostics or secular humanists."[7]

With the expected further decline in vocations, the two Jesuit theologians added, a proportion of one priest to 1,000 American Catholics can be expected for 1985. To give the Catholic student on the secular or uncommitted campus even that much access to a clergyman of their faith would mean an immense expansion of the full-time Newman clerical apostolate to 2,360.

Where could so many priests be found? Michael Novak was not alone in suggesting[8] that miracles might be worked at "New York University which, with its 10,000 Catholic students, is the largest Catholic university in the world,"[9] if "the 89 priests and brothers who care for 6,000 students at Notre Dame, or the 70 Jesuits who have 1,200 students at Holy Cross College" were to be assigned as NYU Newman chaplains.

How many, even of the Catholics, showed any interest in Newman clubs? Mr. Novak used William J. Whalen's contemporary paperback, *Catholics on Campus,* for a statistic on that: one Catholic in five was joining Catholic clubs, or 100,000 out of 500,000. Thus more than the whole Catholic college registration of 300,000 were remaining untouched by the Newman effort.

As an instrument for converting intellectual America, the Newman work was slight. Even as a device for defending the family faith of Catholic students on the secular campuses it was weak, though refinanced and growing. But a central fact was sure: the bulk of the educated laity of the next generation, however slight its contact with formal instruction, would come from the uncommitted campus. It would be literate and scholarly. It would thrust American Catholicism forward toward the greatest intellectual and civic involvement and service in its several-century history.

TEN

Found: The Catholic Writers?

A group of editors of *Commonweal,* one quiet day in the late 1930s, swapped ideas about the American Catholic press. It was about the time that the pro-Franco Michael Williams had lost control of the hand-to-mouth *Commonweal* operation. A handful of progressives including Edward Simeon Skillin, late of Williams College, had taken over.

The chatter turned to the piles of gray copy which *Commonweal* received each week from the bishops' news agency, the marathon-named National Catholic Welfare Conference News Service. The hundred-odd Catholic weeklies of the country were paste-ups from NCWC, the "Commonwealers" agreed. The one open question was whether editors shut their eyes, snatched 10 percent of the pile, and published that, along with the inevitable pictures and speech texts of the local bishop.

"All I know," said one of the *Commonweal* men, "is that it is easy to sketch 'A Portrait of the American Catholic Reader, as Reflected in the Pages of His Papers.' "

He pointed out that *The Tablet* of Brooklyn was a

dominant voice in the chorus of New York Catholic journalism, that Stalin was a menace never far from the minds of communion breakfast speakers of the era, that the Fighting Irish of South Bend, Indiana, were glorious perpetual candidates for the collegiate national football championship and that the harassed advertising directors of Catholic publications were, for some reason, able to count on the sympathies of peddlers of medical home remedies.

"It's clear," said the editor. "The typical American Catholic reader, as mirrored in his diocesan newspaper, feels strongly on the subject of the Brooklyn [baseball] Dodgers. He sets great store by the Notre Dame eleven. He is much opposed to Communism. And he has dry skin and a hernia. However he's not worried about the latter two. He knows he will find a remedy in the pages of his church paper."

That was about the time that the new team at *Commonweal* ran an editorial, a month after their take-over, saying that atrocities were being committed on both sides in the Spanish Civil War, that religion could not be imposed by machine-gun fire, and that it was disturbing to see that the poor in Spain were largely on the anti-Franco side. *Commonweal*'s circulation dropped 25 percent at once. Almost all the clergy readers canceled their subscriptions. The country's one lay-edited Catholic journal of opinion bade fair to vanish before it was many more weeks older.

Yet *Commonweal* survived, thanks perhaps to the fact that its editors were too prudent to follow up their doubts about the new Catholic military dictator of Spain with snide remarks about Notre Dame football or Brooklyn's Bums. When times got very hard *Commonweal* knew where to find 200 or 300 angels with $50 each to support a budget which, even in the middle sixties, was only $225,000 a year. In 1964 *Commonweal*, then old and respected although still earnestly liberal, enjoyed a circulation of 41,500, all but a sixth of it Catholic.

Commonweal, on occasion, has been praised as "the most distinguished journal of Catholic opinion in the English-speaking world." It offered a good example both of the opportunities and of the problems faced by laymen in America as they assumed new responsibilities in the post-Vatican II Church.

As the lay-edited *Commonweal* saw it, papal and episcopal authority was central to Catholicism but was also answerable to the "public opinion in the Church," which Pope Pius XII and other ecclesiastical leaders and council Fathers extolled from 1950 onward. In the view of James O'Gara, *Commonweal's* managing editor, and his associate, John Leo, a syndicated columnist of the Catholic press, that meant that lay writers need not hesitate to attack actions of such eminent churchmen as New York's Cardinal Francis Spellman, the virtual primate of the United States Catholic Church, or even of the pope himself.

When Pope Paul VI symbolically placed his pontifical tiara on the high altar of St. Peter's as a gift to the poverty-stricken hundreds of millions of the world, John Leo, forty-five years the junior of Cardinal Spellman, was indignant to see it wind up as a possession of the New York prelate, a famous collector of ecclesiastical souvenirs.

The cook at the Waldorf-Astoria carried the tiara out from his kitchen in a brown paper bag, the eloquent young Turk of Catholic syndicated journalism told his readership in a scathing description of the occasion on which the aging New York churchman revealed his new acquisition. The explanation that the tiara was an expression of gratitude for American aid to the poor of the planet and that it would become the property of the American national cathedral in Washington did nothing to mollify Mr. Leo, nor did he seem abashed when clergy said that the bits about the paper bag and the chef were inaccurate.

An example of how free *Commonweal* felt about criticizing the pope was provided on October 1, 1965. Managing editor O'Gara found signs that Pope Paul was moving back away from Pope John's "open window." He said:

> I am sure that such comments on the pope [are] never [supposed to] be made, at least by a faithful son of the Church. But this notion, I believe . . . belongs to an earlier era. . . . Well-being of the Church demands from us the most scrupulous kind of honesty and plain speaking, and honesty requires the flat statement that in recent weeks Pope Paul's words can have brought comfort only to the traditionalists in the council and throughout the world. . . . The council can turn its back on the future and return to the mentality of the ghetto: timid, afraid, choosing to live on the capital of the past and condemning all that is new . . . or the council can turn to the future unafraid and determined to show how wrong they are who say that the Church is irrelevant. . . . Is there any real doubt as to which course should be followed?

Commonweal's remarks brought letters accusing the editors of an attempt to undermine papal leadership, a Roman Catholic cornerstone. In the October 15, 1965, issue the editors jointly denied the charge:

> We were . . . distressed and confused. That seemed to us a perfectly good reason to complain. Is it disrespectful to be confused? Is it rebellious to be distressed? Is it arrogant to find apparent discrepancies between Paul's statements and conciliar documents? . . . It is possible to take an encyclical with full seriousness and respect as an important instrument of the Church's Magisterium [teaching authority], and yet directly and bluntly, though not capriciously and irresponsibly, criticize its deficiencies. . . . It is the kind of respect responsible adults pay to other responsible adults, regardless of the difference of rank between them. . . . There will be no genuine, continuing renewal in the Church unless it is perfectly legitimate for those subject to authority to point out the failures of Authority. . . . We would have done neither the Church nor the pope a service by failing to say so.

FOUND: THE CATHOLIC WRITERS?

An assertive lay voice was something new in American Catholic life, and by no means all of those who scanned the expanding liberal wing of American Catholic journalism (nearly all the magazines, and a small but growing share of the diocesan weekly newspapers) liked what they saw. Perhaps surprisingly, laymen were often among those who objected most vigorously as they watched fixed attitudes dissolve before an apparently anarchic trend. *Commonweal,* ever since the first gingerly anti-Franco days, had found many such letters in the postman's sack. On October 30, 1965, happy to share a joke, *Commonweal's* lay editors ran a house ad headlined, "People are raving about *Commonweal.*" These "raves" were listed:

"I wouldn't have your miserable, lying rag if you gave it away. Anonymous."

"As a pastor I'll forbid it in my pamphlet rack, as a bishop I'll forbid it in my diocese. Parish priest, Washington, D.C." [*Commonweal's* in-joke was that their career-minded correspondent was assuming promotions which were by no means certain.]

"I have no desire to receive a magazine which retards the spread of the Faith. Monsignor, Maryland."

"Your fine Catholic Communist magazine has but one prayer from me, and that is that you and your like are out of business at once. Anonymous, Boston, Mass."

"I am unable to tell your line from the Communist Party line. Cancel my subscription. Patriot."

Commonweal invited readers to give themselves "leverage," to subscribe so that they would have something to cancel.

Even if all the letters that week were staff-written, as they sounded, they summarized many man-in-the-pew and priest-in-the-rectory sentiments with regard to *Commonweal* and other Catholic periodicals: the nosy and sometimes scandal-mongering but often brilliant *The National Catholic Reporter,* the far leftist *Catholic Worker, Ramparts, U.S.*

FOUND: THE CATHOLIC WRITERS?

Catholic, Jubilee, The Sign, The Critic, The Catholic World of the Paulists, *Liguorian, Ave Maria* of Notre Dame University, the *Delmarva* (diocesan) *Dialog* of Delaware, the Camden, New Jersey, *Catholic Star Herald, The Pilot* of Boston, *Criterion* of Indianapolis, *The Pittsburgh Catholic,* Rhode Island's *Providence Visitor,* and *America.*

In all of these the causes of justice for the Negro, of aid to the poor of the world, and of good relations with non-Catholics (ecumenism) were promoted. A worry about Vietnam bordering on total pacifism infiltrated some. The spirit of "we have ours, let's forget those next in line" found sympathy in none. But what was true of editors was by no means always so among readers. Some would have gladly "stopped the world." The immigrants of the 1800s were now in the middle class and would have preferred to freeze life as they found it with a minimum of foreign aid, a minimum of foreign relations, an occasional atom bomb exploded atop national enemies perhaps, and a stern hand with colored troublemakers. One epithet leaped to the mind of many of these as they complained to lay and clerical editors alike: "Communist." Somehow, a legion of these objectors were convinced that communism had spun its way into the heads of too many Church editors, clerics and laymen alike. Their correspondence made some of the liveliest reading in Church periodicals:

"U.S. Catholic mag. rag stinks. I wouldn't have it in my home. Mrs. L. Murphy, Whittier, Calif." [*U.S. Catholic* magazine, November, 1964.]

"Please cancel . . . subscription. . . . I am in complete disagreement with your Leftist policy, your so-called liberal policy. . . . [The writer punctuated this with a quotation from a 1906 sermon by a Father Bernard Vaughan who had said that "liberal Catholics" were enemy "weapons with which to stab at the heart of our Church"]. James J. O'Connell Sr., Chicago." [Same issue of *U.S. Catholic.*]

"I find your magazine the most disgusting Catholic magazine I have ever read. In several . . . issues about all you have mentioned is SEX! . . . : 'Sane Sidelights on Sex,' 'Home Background for Sex Instruction!' I am beginning to wonder if the Communists are behind all this rot. In the August issue there was an article asking how to confess sins of impurity. . . . I was just plain shocked. . . . You should have told that girl she shouldn't be committing sins of impurity in the first place. . . . J. R." [*Liguorian,* November, 1965.]

"I thought that 'Ave Maria' was a magazine devoted to the Blessed Virgin. Reading the last issue I found the name of Mary on the front cover only, 'Ave Maria.' So please stop my subscription. To hear criticism of our ecclesiastical authorities, I have enough with the secular press. Father Damian Gobeo, Louisiana." [*Ave Maria,* April 9, 1966.]

The *St. Louis Review,* which is high on the list of the country's most liberal diocesan weeklies, probed repeatedly into the world poverty problem and into the internal Catholic controversy over birth control and the woman's "safe period" until one reader proposed sarcastically that it change its name to "The St. Louis Rhythm and Blues."[1]

Sometimes letters were wistful. One writer wanted only to be comforted when he opened the pages of a religious magazine. Rather than solace, he complained, he found the same frightening woes which leaped from secular headlines. Often, however, the battlers against Catholic liberalism used a self-assured and stormy rhetoric, as in the case of one correspondent who wrote to the feisty *Delmarva Dialog* to object to a John Leo column. In this case the young Mr. Leo had criticized Cardinal Spellman's aides for the sudden brief exiling in 1965 of the pacifist Jesuit, Father Daniel Berrigan, who had objected to prosecution of the Vietnam war. Mr. Leo wrote that Father Berrigan, a tutor of the draft card burner, David Miller of *The Catholic Worker,* was "one of the most Christ-like men I have ever met."[2]

"I don't believe," said the infuriated letter writer, "that John Leo would recognize a Christ-like man if one spit in his eye."

That, said *The Catholic Report*, "wins our newly established award for the most vivid polemical image of the month."[3]

The conservative letter writers were not wholly without publications which flattered their views, even though Ed Skillin in the middle sixties took the view as *Commonweal*'s editor that his sole reason for omitting conservatives was that he could find none who were intelligent. The century-old *Wanderer* of St. Paul, lay-edited from its inception, cried out week after week against communism in all its real and imagined forms, decried the "Liberal Establishment," and lamented American involvement with the United Nations and the rest of the world. *The Tablet* of Brooklyn, under the editorship of the aged Patrick F. Scanlan, reminisced about the days earlier in the century when eight grades of schooling were enough for a man, and had no apologies for its past America First, Coughlinite and McCarthyist sympathies. In the early days of the American Catholic ghetto *The Tablet* had been a cannon firing at President Roosevelt, New York's progressive governor and Senator Herbert Lehman, and World War II involvement with Britain against Hitler. The salvos kept coming in the middle sixties even though the new bishop of Eastern Long Island, Walter Kellenberg, quietly set up his own rather advanced *Long Island Catholic* to wean away *Tablet* readers. At the same time publications like *The Sign* scolded Mr. Scanlan and his weekly by name. When Pope Paul VI visited the United Nations in October, 1964, Father Ralph Gorman, the editor of *Sign*, protested that *The Tablet*'s Mr. Scanlan refused to give up his isolationist dream of a "UN out of the US, and a US out of the UN." Mr. Scanlan, he said, "cagily" clung to his anti-UN bias in the face of patent papal approval by asking this question:

"One now wonders what will be the result. Will an end be put to the failures of the last twenty years . . . ? Will unselfish and consistent campaigns for peace be carried out or will . . . the anti-Western combinations . . . and other factors, including the starting of forty military actions since the peace organization was formed, continue?"

That shook loose a new volley of letters. Joseph Roberts, of Floral Park, Queens, in *The Tablet's* diocese, told Father Gorman that he was a thirty-year reader of both *The Sign* and *The Tablet,* that he believed he should support "the Catholic press, especially that segment which is intelligently militant in defense of my Faith," and that he trusted that he would never again see the Passionist magazine "airing . . . differences with an official diocesan paper such as *The Tablet.*"

Layman Scanlan, between Mr. Roberts' lines, seemed to take on bits of papal infallibility even where his hostility to the UN was concerned. Father Gorman assured Mr. Roberts that *The Sign's* repudiation of Mr. Scanlan's isolationism was thorough and not at all withdrawn.

The civil war raging in the middle sixties between liberal lay and clerical editors, on the one hand, and bewildered and outraged conservative readers, on the other, was fought on new theological terrain provided by Vatican Council II. The skirmishing tested how great a role laymen would play inside the church reformed by the late, great Pope John. Some lay editors startled bishops by their audacity. When Archbishop Egidio Vagnozzi, the Apostolic Delegate to Washington, sent a confidential letter to the 250 bishops of this country telling them that it was the wish of "the Holy See" that there be no further interfaith religious services pending additional studies by a Rome commission, Robert Hoyt, the dauntless editor of *National Catholic Reporter,* published the embarrassing missive. Mr. Hoyt described the episode to fellow Catholic editors later. He said that, as an

161

American, he would, for example, expose any "confidential" message from "the White House" asking district attorneys to suspend portions of the 1964 Civil Rights Act pending efforts to smooth white Mississippian feelings. Some unnamed persons had accused him of "opening the private mail of the bishops and interfering in the line of communication between the pope and his brother [prelates], but, he said, he felt that the parallel with the mythical (and unthinkable) White House case was exact. Sometimes, said Mr. Hoyt, difficult decisions must be made by a Catholic editor. "Asking permission to publish" was, he said, *not* that sort of an agonizing decision. His conscience was his guide. A few years earlier the revelation of such a directive of the Apostolic Delegation or even the admission that such communications took place would have been unthinkable inside the American Catholic press.

This writer asked Robert Hoyt, as one of the most controversial of the new American Catholic lay editors, how he would sum up reaction to his type of candid, searching editing: newswork which spared not even the Holy See as it pried for the truth.

"Some," he replied, "say in effect that it's about time. Some are shocked to their ankle bones. Others have hardly noticed what's happening."

Bob Hoyt's *The National Catholic Reporter* was founded in October, 1964, as a nonprofit lay enterprise, financed indirectly during its first months by a parallel publication, the Kansas City diocesan *The Catholic Reporter,* of which Hoyt was also editor. The bishop of Kansas City, Charles H. Helmsing, a leading progressive inside the American hierarchy, and an advocate of a more vocal lay role, was in one way or another the angel of both publications.

The National Catholic Reporter was launched on the fourth anniversary of the diocesan *Catholic Reporter.* In one year it zoomed from a circulation of 11,000 to 50,000. An analysis of its readership was done in May and June of 1965 by the John T. McLean market consulting organization, and provided an interesting insight into the new readership opening up to American Catholic editors.[4] Sixty-two percent subscribed by mail and, hence, were easily available for analyses. Of this 62 percent:

Clergy accounted for 15.91 percent, many times more than their share of the American Catholic population.

Sisters represented 13.94 percent, a remarkable indication of how alert the convents of the country are to Pope John's and Vatican II's *aggiornamento* or updating.

Laymen made up 32.11 percent.

The marketing consultants wrote to 2,371 of the laymen mail subscribers and received answers from just under half. This sampling produced fascinating evidence of the emergence of a new, highly literate American Catholic lay audience:

Seventy-one percent were college graduates.

Thirty-four percent had master's degrees.

An almost unbelievable 16 percent had doctorates or other advanced professional degrees.

Mr. Hoyt's readers clearly were among those who would lead the American Catholicism of the next generation.

By contrast Sister Mary Paul Paye found the following when she conducted a research project during March–May, 1962, on diocesan newspaper readership. Her effort was part of her work for a doctorate in mass communications at Syracuse University.[5] Sister chose a paper with a circulation of 10,000, about equally divided between back-of-the-church sales and subscriptions. She wrote to 140 subscribers and received answers from two thirds. These were the results:

Eight percent gave no replies.

Four percent said that they had never attended high school and that they gave 100 percent approval to the contents of the diocesan organ.

Forty-six percent had some high school but no college training. Seventy-two percent of these approved the Church paper.

Forty-two percent had received at least some college training. Only 34 percent of them wholly endorsed the diocesan publication. Of this 34 percent, 25 percent were women and only 9 percent men.

The picture of a still poorly instructed but progressively better educated laity was quite as clear as an additional consideration. Alienation from the old-style reticent "house organ" Church publication proceeded with each forward step on the way to higher education, with men (the fathers of the families) leading the way as those most disaffected.

If the lay reader of the yesteryear-type Church publication was restless, the new wave of liberal lay editors was equally rambunctious. *Ramparts,* a California slick monthly, published and edited by Edward M. Keating, a Catholic convert, rebuked Los Angeles' Cardinal J. Francis A. McIntyre for too halfhearted an interest in Negro justice and for generally arch-conservative policies. It campaigned in behalf of Rolf Hochhuth's right to put on his play, *The Deputy,* a violent assault on Pope Pius XII as a passive bystander during Hitler's murder of six million Jews. It devoted the whole November, 1964, issue to the scandal of civil rights murders in Mississippi, helping pave the way for federal prosecutions. It demanded more vigorous White House peace efforts in Vietnam. To legions of Catholic laity of the old stripe, and to many clergy, this was an American Catholicism of an unrecognizable new type.

I asked Edward Keating a few questions about *Ramparts.* I

pointed out that his young magazine in the middle sixties was making a notable impression on evolving American Catholic journalism. The reply from the battling publisher was in character. He wrote:

> I disagree with you that I have a significant impact on Catholic publishing, except possibly in the sense that since the Catholic publishing extravaganza in this country cannot silence me, they do the next best thing by generally remaining silent about me and *Ramparts,* a situation that leaves me completely unmoved, since it is not the orthodox and pietistic Catholic that I seek to reach. . . .

Was *Ramparts* a lay Catholic publication or in any sense "Catholic"? What was it trying to do? What did it see as the rights of the Magisterium, the papal and hierarchical teaching authority? The answer was spirited:

> *Ramparts* has no specific goal. . . . I personally consider *Ramparts* to be a Catholic publication.
>
> However, there exists in Catholic publishing, and indeed throughout most of the Church, the spirit of Triumphalism, i.e., All Roads Lead to Rome, Go Directly to Rome, Do Not Pass Go, Do Not Collect 200 Days' Indulgences.
>
> The world of today is not the world of five or ten years ago, and men are out of joint; a multiphased revolution is taking place that can best be summarized by saying that we are in a human revolution wherein for the first time in history, really, attention is being focused on the individual human being who lives in this time and place, not the human being who is an abstraction that is created by the scholastic and neo-scholastic mind.
>
> You asked me questions, now I ask you a question: what is a Catholic publication? I honestly do not know the answer to that question. A Catholic is a Christian theoretically, and a Christian theoretically is one who loves his fellow man. But having said that I find it difficult to distinguish between a Christian and a member of any other religious community.
>
> But then there are Catholics and Catholics: Pope John XXIII is listed on the books as a Catholic and so, mysteriously, is Pope Paul

FOUND: THE CATHOLIC WRITERS?

VI; Cardinal McIntyre is also on the masthead as is the Negro Catholic who suffers because of his co-religionist in Louisiana and elsewhere in the world.

I have on my desk a photograph of a Negro priest in the Southern diocese. His bishop, also a registered Catholic, is an out and out racist who feels more at home with a red neck atheistic White bigot than he would with his own priest on whom he placed his episcopal hand at ordination. Therefore, if you ask what is a Catholic publication, I must ask you in turn what is a Catholic?

Our battles are wherever we find ourselves. The battle lines are generally drawn against the establishment, whatever its nature. *Ramparts* is essentially anti-establishment . . . because of the fact that the establishment (s) need analysis and criticism, if not out-right repudiation because it is the establishment (s) that have moved man and history to this brink of utter disaster not only in temporal terms but in spiritual as well. . . . What we are battling for is the individual human being. . . .

The role of candid self-examination in the Catholic press?

It is the sine qua non of a viable existence. . . . The Catholic press by and large plays hierarchical games under the tutelage of local bishops. We have a controlled press and no controlled press will honestly and candidly criticize itself. The diocesan newspapers are the propaganda playthings of 120 bishops in this country who have not the slightest idea of what a newspaper should be. The diocesan newspaper is as much a part of the bishop's office as his episcopal ring which is nothing but a hangover from a paranoiac past.

The rights of the Magisterium?

I can only say that when someone can definitely tell me what the Magisterium is, without a lot of nonsense and doubletalk, I will be able to answer. . . . The very presence of the concept of the Magisterium comes close to heresy since it violates the canon law which places the primacy of conscience above everything else, something that most bishops and popes do not begin to understand. A publication that presents a balanced pro and con on every subject ends up a cipher. . . .

Mr. Keating added that *Ramparts*, a periodical which had been planned as "a little Catholic literary quarterly" with a fall 1964 circulation of 3,000, had "for some extraordinary reason exploded into a national monthly magazine" of 40,000 copies in less than a year.

Ducking fights and blind adherence to tradition had been no part of his strangely successful formula, Mr. Keating made clear. That not every fellow Catholic editor admired his efforts was, however, evident. Father Ralph Gorman editorialized in *The Sign* in December, 1965: "A West Coast magazine edited by laymen has pictured members of the hierarchy as if they were a combination of Hitler, Mussolini and Satan. This publication declares itself 'fiercely independent.' It is, indeed, but independent of maturity and good taste."

However justified some of *The Sign*'s criticism of details of the *Ramparts* experiment, there was no question but that Edward Keating and the other newly arrived rebels in the Catholic or neo-Catholic journalists' ranks were supported by much contemporary philosophizing about the Church, the press and the world.

John J. Deedy, Jr., of *The Pittsburgh Catholic*, pointed out, for instance, at the Washington, D.C., convention of the National Council of Catholic Women, November 11–14, 1964: "Pope John [said] in a brief, neglected observation to Italian newsmen that, in some ways, contains more wisdom than the entire Decree on Communications adopted by Vatican Council II: 'The Catholic journalist must be prepared to *defend truth, justice and honesty even before religion and the Gospels.*'"

Something similar was uttered by Vienna's Cardinal Francis Koenig at a meeting of Catholic newsmen in Assisi in

Italy in November, 1965, just before the end of Vatican Council II. He said:

> That public opinion holds a rightful place in the Church, no less a person than Pope Pius XII has drawn to our attention. . . . Public opinion in the Church is especially the opinion of the laity. . . . The Catholic layman has in a certain manner, in fact we should say especially, the Catholic journalist as his spokesman.
>
> The Church has called the layman to his co-responsibility. If the layman makes use of the right that falls to him, and if the Catholic journalist, as the spokesman of the laity, makes use of this right in certain manners and with certain methods which sometimes surprise, nay even astonish the Catholic hierarchy, we must also find there a proof of the vitality of the Church. . . .
>
> If the Catholic journalist has something to say, he must not content himself with waiting for the sign from the bishop, nor for news from Rome; he must warn when he thinks warning is necessary; he must stimulate where he thinks there must be stimulation; he must inform the world about the Church and the Church about the world. . . . Thus the Church speaks today to the world, but the world also to the Church.[6]

Robert Hoyt's *The National Catholic Reporter* said on its first anniversary in October, 1965, that its idea of a lay-edited Catholic paper had been summed up precisely by Father John Courtney Murray, the Maryland Jesuit who wrote much of Vatican II's strong statement on the need for religious liberty in all countries, Catholic and non-Catholic alike. Father Murray shortly before had made his comment at a two-day Catholic press symposium in Rome. He said: "The Catholic press does not exist in order to create a public image of the Church that will be untrue to the reality of the Pilgrim Church, the Wayfaring Church, the Church that trudges along the road of history and gets its feet dusty at times, the Church that has hands by which she takes hold of the dirty stuff of history because history is rather dirty stuff. . . .

The National Catholic Reporter added, in its birthday anniversary statement: "As for criticism of authority, Father Murray acknowledges that freedom creates no right in the Catholic press to stand against Church authority; 'it does, however, create a responsibility to note abuses of authority, and thus to serve the true interests of authority.'"

This was all a far cry from other years when Church officials seemed to have no use for a vigorous press of whatever kind, secular or ecclesiastical.

Monsignor Yzermans, the spokesman for the American hierarchy in 1966, commented: "I've been at meetings of priests where they picked the press apart, saying for instance 'I was there; the paper says there were 40 people, there were only 37!' Part of it was caused by the feeling 'what did we ever get from the press?'; that the press was hostile. Some of it is specifically Irish. In Ireland 100 years ago the press belonged to the establishment and the establishment was Protestant."

Monsignor Yzermans was of "the new breed," or at least the "transitional breed," as he called priests born around 1930 and formed in the seminary just before Vatican II and the great reform known as the New Theology. In Notre Dame's *Ave Maria* he pointed out on May 8, 1965, that Dr. Robert Root, director of the Department of Religious Journalism at Syracuse University, had made this comment on the difficult relationship between churchmen and reporters: "If journalists are sometimes unreasonable in thinking officials of Church and State should hold all sessions in goldfish bowls, religious leaders are just as unrealistic if they feel those who have risen in church power structures possess some divine right to decide what the common people may hear."

Monsignor Yzermans agreed. He said: "I feel that the Catholic Church could profit today from a few more goldfish bowls. . . . The right to information . . . admittedly is scandalously ignored in many areas of Church administration today. . . . Let us be honest. In the Church today there are many dangers to healthy public opinion. The cleric endowed with the siege mentality as well as the layman with the pay-and-pray complex are serious threats to healthy public opinion."

The average Catholic layman in the late sixties of the twentieth century was not much of a reader of Catholic publications. At the typical parish church, Masses ended without a soul taking notice of the pamphlet racks or the piles of the diocesan paper in the vestibule. *The Catholic World*, reviewing Edward M. Keating's *The Scandal of Silence*,[7] speculated that Mr. Keating may have guessed too high in judging that only one in five subscribers to a diocesan paper even looked at it.

"My bishop wants subscriptions to the diocese paper," the local pastor told me in Springfield, Vermont. "I sent in 270 of them, and paid for three-quarters myself. I sent them to people who needed it. Some wrote saying 'stop'!"

In the middle sixties, according to *The Catholic Press Annual,* there were 141 Catholic newspapers with a circulation of 4,672,476 in North America—the lion's share in the United States, not quite one copy for every ten American Catholics. There were 478 Catholic magazines with a total of 20,910,294 copies. The American Catholic press accounted for roughly half the country's religious periodicals. Robert Hoyt calculated the combined budgets of Catholic and all other religious periodicals in the United States at several "hundreds of millions of dollars" a year, but Mr. Hoyt, for one, was dismayed with what the churches got for such an outlay. Robert Lekachman in *The Religious Press in America* judged that only six publications of the whole American religious press (two of them Catholic, *Commonweal* and *America,* and four others—*Christian Century, Christianity and Crisis, Commentary* and *Midstream*) had anything of value to say to those outside their faiths as fellow humans, and that even these struck no "clear religious note" in the discussion of world affairs beyond some sectarian special pleading.[8]

What was wrong? When Gerald E. Sherry resigned in the middle sixties as the editor of *The Georgia Bulletin* of Atlanta, a sprightly diocesan paper published under the auspices of the progressive Archbishop Paul J. Hallinan, I asked Sherry to sketch his story as a veteran of one and one-half decades of layman service in the American Catholic press. He answered that he was the son of middle-class British parents from Lancashire, England, that he had become "a liberal crusader" as a Catholic soap box orator at sixteen or seventeen, and that his first audiences in Liverpool and London ranged "from no one to several thousand." He added:

I have never had any difficulty with such things as Divine Revelation, Church authority and the like. . . .

The funny thing is that I have worked for four bishops, three of whom were as conservative as you can find. . . . Yet I, as an unabashed liberal . . . could garner respect from them. . . . In the fifteen years [I have had] in the Catholic press, I have never been censored in what I wrote by any bishop. O, the Apostolic Delegate has occasionally queried my bosses as to my orthodoxy but it has never been on essentials. It appears Delegates' queries were based on what other people told them, not on what I actually said or did. . . .

Yet Gerry Sherry quit to edit a West Virginia secular daily. Why? He went on:

The Catholic press is not servile, it is merely deficient of professional journalists, well versed in their religion and committed to it. . . . In my opinion the Catholic press as such can never have influence on American intellectuals because it is not an educated press. . . .

We require more editors . . . aware of history and theology. Few are willing to make the sacrifices involved. I know of no (Ameri-

171

can) Catholic publication that could be called outstanding. And I am most disappointed in the trend of the only decent national Catholic weekly of any importance, *The National Catholic Reporter*. This paper has the opportunity to be great (and it has an educated staff) but they have a basic negative attitude to the past and an indiscreet opinion of the present. What is more they lack Christian optimism for the future.

I suppose the best of the Catholic press can be numbered on one hand: *The Pilot* of Boston, *Criterion* of Indianapolis, *The Review* of St. Louis, *The Catholic Review* of Baltimore, *The Universe Bulletin* of Cleveland.

Of course, you can add *The Catholic Reporter* of Kansas and, I like to think, my own paper [*The Georgia Bulletin*] which has an influence in this Southern community far out of proportion to the one percent of the secular population that we represent. . . . In the papers I have mentioned there is a certain intellectual value but none of us compare with the great European (Catholic) newspapers such as *The Catholic Herald* of London, and *The Croix* of Paris. . . .

"*America* . . . has become a mediocrity. . . . *Commonweal* has . . . a much greater intellectual depth. . . . *The Wanderer* . . . is a rabid, ultra-conservative rag which has no depth and is almost solely political in content. It has great support in Catholic American traditionalist circles because of its great stress on negative anti-Communism and its opposition to social justice in contrast to what is required by Catholic principles."

Gerry Sherry's was a sad swan song for a distinguished Church journalistic career. Was the picture of Catholic press effort, lay and clerical, quite that dismal? I did not think so. To me the true measuring rod was the relationship of Catholics to the widest world of American letters. In one generation Eugene O'Neill, F. Scott Fitzgerald, John O'Hara, Theodore Dreiser, Mary McCarthy (*Memories of a Catholic Girlhood*), James T. Farrell and others turned their backs on their Church and left unlamenting and unlamented. By the middle sixties, at least, their departure was mourned. When *Commonweal* sought someone to review W. A. Swanberg's *Theodore Dreiser* it was proud to get James T. Farrell (who attacked the author for long descriptions of Dreiser as a woman-chaser, and insisted that Dreiser's great art was what counted).[9] When Dr. Henry Dan Piper published *F. Scott Fitzgerald: a Critical Portrait, The Catholic News* of New York provided space for an affectionate, possessive review.[10]

More importantly a new, frank articulate group of writers who were at home both in the faith and in the world of letters began to appear in the sixties, a generation involved both in the Church press and, more importantly, in the outer world of letters: Phyllis McGinley, a Pulitzer Prize winner; Flannery O'Connor, the novelist; Jean and Walter Kerr, the playwright and the play critic; J. F. Powers, Edwin O'Connor, Wilfrid Sheed, Paul Horgan, Daniel Callahan, Michael Novak, John Leo, John Cogley, Philip Scharper, James O'Gara. The list was still short but it was growing. A generation of responsible artful writers at ease in the world and in their Church at last was at hand. Some degree of a reforming impact on Catholicism and on America was a sure future consequence.

ELEVEN

New Organizations and Old

In an era of an ever better instructed Catholic layman the irony was that the choice of Church organizations open to absorb his energies and talents was, as wide as it was, almost uniformly, unattractive.

Martin Work, the former advertising agency man and United States Army colonel, who was executive director of the hierarchy's National Council of Catholic Men, made this estimate in 1960 in an article in *The Sign:* there were 100,000 American Catholic organizations, one for every 400 or 500 Catholics. How limp and drab many of these were could be seen reflected in a comment by Father Edward S. Stanton, a Jesuit, in an article in *America* on February 2, 1963. He wrote: "College graduates are, in the eyes of a large number of priests, 'the most uncooperative people in the parish.'" As director of the Boston Priests' Sodality and as a former teacher of theology at the Jesuits' Boston and Holy Cross colleges, Father Stanton was in a position to know the story from both sides.

The heart of the problem was that the familiar organizations of American Catholic life, the Holy Name Society for men, the Knights of Columbus, the St. Vincent de Paul Society, the Rosary and Altar Society, were dead, at least in their old forms. Aimed at the fostering of personal piety inside a small Catholic world cut off from the broader American society, these old groupings had to change radically, raising levels of community consciousness and of intellectual interest, or they had to reconcile themselves to senescence and disintegration.

Happily, a collection of new organizations began to develop at the uphill side of the older ones. Some, like the Christian Family Movement which began in Chicago in 1943 in a bull session among a half-dozen layman lawyers, insurance agents, businessmen and ex-seminarians, boasted by 1964 of an incredibly expanded membership: 40,000 married couple members in the United States, 5,000 more in Canada, 30,000 in Latin America, "perhaps" another 30,000 in forty-five other countries.

Others were tiny but not, for that reason, insignificant such as AID (the Association for International Development) of Paterson, New Jersey, which cooperated with Seton Hall University of Newark in training college graduates for work abroad in the Peace Corps and in other foreign assistance groups, adding a specific spiritual and religious inspiration to the salaried efforts of the members. In the middle sixties AID reported that it was still minuscule ("9 single men, 35 married men, 35 married women and 91 children"), but at least a few were demonstrating how the generous principles of such encyclicals as those of Pope John XXIII could be lived practically in American lives.

The organization which best illustrated the problems of American Catholic organizational life at the dawn of an era of greater lay involvement in Church life and work was the Knights of Columbus, by all odds the best financed of the

Catholic lay groups. The K of C had been born in 1882 in the basement of St. Mary's Church in New Haven and could not have hoped for a more magnificent material fruition. A young curate, Father Michael J. McGivney (in a New Haven dominated by the Yankees' Yale University, and laced with uneasiness about Irish and other immigrants), had an inspiration: an association which could provide its hard-pressed members with life insurance and fellowship, plus some religious encouragement. The memory of signs at hiring windows, "No Irish Need Apply," was vivid in the New Haven of those days, but no such banner was hoisted over the heads of the new K of C. In fact, those who signed the charter with Father McGivney seemed to be exclusively Irish: Matthew C. O'Connor, Cornelius T. Driscoll, James T. Mullen, John T. Kerrigan, Daniel Colwell and William M. Geary.

Some good works were always part of the K of C program, but essentially the society saw to it, through the insurance program, that deceased members were interred and that at least a little something went to widows and orphaned children. By 1964 the K of C had paid out $160,795,000 in insurance benefits, and had another $1,340,902,358 in policies in force.

The K of C prided itself on a $900,000-a-year advertising campaign in secular communications media replying to attacks against the Catholic religion and offering instruction to prospective converts. By the middle sixties about 35,000 persons a year signed up for the religion courses. There was no other convert program quite like it, and bishops and priests expressed admiration. But beer, pretzels, clambakes and card games in the 5,000 "councils" were the core of the K of C for many. As one recruiting folder put it:

Members of the Knights of Columbus, of course, do not spend every minute of every shining hour dashing frantically hither and yon on errands of mercy and kindness. No normal man can be serious all the time; habitual solemnity wears him down so that he is not much good to himself or anyone else.

In every council of the order there is one officer responsible for arranging "good time" programs that all members will enjoy. Some noise, some laughter, a well spread table and a good song—these are things men like, things knights frequently enjoy in their councils.

Some critics of the K of C at the bishops' secretariat at 1312 Massachusetts Avenue Northwest in Washington, D.C. (the National Catholic Welfare Conference), tried to be realistic in appraising Father McGivney's remarkable organization, and summed it up privately this way: "The Masons wouldn't let them in so the Catholics formed their own Masons."

Along with the "good times," however, went the provision that members had to be "practical Catholics." There were regulations calling for the expulsion of religious backsliders. But how often such rules were invoked, if ever, was rarely discussed, if at all.

Whatever its weaknesses in the intellectual and apostolic fields the K of C continued into the sixties to prosper numerically and financially. On June 30, 1964, the K of C reported assets of $237,221,643, and a membership of 1,165,466 in all states of the union, in all ten Canadian provinces and in Mexico, Puerto Rico, the Canal Zone and the Philippines. The most important share of the membership, that part which held K of C life insurance, stood at 441,566. The supreme knight was Dr. John D. McDevitt, former superintendent of schools in Waltham, Massachusetts, and a Master of Arts from Boston College, who had two honorary doctorates (from St. Michael's College, Winooski, Vermont, and from St. Francis College, Biddeford, Maine).

The trouble facing Father McGivney's knights in the mid-sixties was indicated by repeated cases of blackballing of Negro applicants for membership. The ecumenical council hammered home the message that racial differences were unimportant in God's eyes, but time after time black men of the Catholic faith found themselves rejected for K of C membership. Joseph Bertrand, a star athlete at Notre Dame

University, was turned down by Loop Council 182 in Chicago. The grand knight, Eugene R. Liner, and five other officials of the order thereupon resigned, charging that racial prejudice had been displayed "openly and fiercely." Auxiliary Bishop Cletus F. O'Donnell agreed. He said that the blackballers had committed a "disgusting and shameful" misdeed. The Jesuits' magazine, *America,* a constant critic of recurring K of C racism, went further. In an editorial in its November 30, 1963, issue, just after the episode, it protested that "it is well known that the 92 [Chicago K of C] councils count not a single Negro among their 40,000 members."

On February 15, 1964, *America* returned to the attack. It praised a new K of C council in Augusta, Georgia, for admitting five Negroes, but it quoted "a priest," as the source of its information that "a prominent Negro Catholic gentleman" who had had a past grand knight as his sponsor was refused membership by at least four Cincinnati councils on six occasions over a ten-year period. "The sabers of the Cincinnati knights are stained with social injustice," the magazine protested.

Even as late as April 28, 1966, the Jesuit review was back to the same theme. This time Charles K. Jackson, a member of the Detroit homicide squad, and a commentator at Old St. Mary's parish, was blackballed at the policemen's Monsignor Flanagan Council 3180, inside the automobile city. Mr. Jackson's sponsor, Vincent Piersante, Detroit's chief of detectives, resigned on the grounds that the turndown was "on the basis of Mr. Jackson's color, and was indefensible and a sad commentary to say the least." The chaplain of the police force, Monsignor Francis X. Canfield, rector of Sacred Heart Seminary, was of the same mind. He said that the racial motivation had been "established beyond cavil." He too gave up K of C membership.[1]

The plumed hats, the sabers, the martial overtones and the grandiose titles which had given a flavor of glory and a sense of strength and protection to the Catholic millhands and laborers of Father McGivney's day continued to be a part of the K of C picture nearly a century later. Sometimes there had been startling negative consequences such as in the era before 1913 when it took a Congressional committee to strike down rumors that the knights were a virulently anti-Protestant sect, pledged by secret oath to "hang, burn and strangle" non-Catholic fellow Christians. For decades the knights offered a reward of $25,000 to anyone who could provide proof of the libel, but the books of harmless secret rituals designed to awe and impress the members continued to be passed from grand knight to grand knight and to be held in strongboxes in the times in between.

As the sixties began, the Knights of Columbus found waves of reform suggestions and criticisms washing in on them from all sides, some complaining about labor relations policies at the New Haven national headquarters where a new twenty-story main building was on the way, some objecting that the K of C was long overdue in making common cause with groups of other faiths and backgrounds in joint community programs.

Auxiliary Bishop Joseph B. Brunini, of Natchez-Jackson, Mississippi, told the knights, for instance, at their New Orleans national convention in 1965:

I would challenge the Knights of Columbus to begin [an ecumenical] dialogue . . . with their neighbors and friends of all races and of all groups. I would challenge them specifically to begin the dialogue with the leaders of the Young Men's Christian Association, and among the great Masonic bodies of our country. Truly the Knights of Columbus will find much in common with these, their brethren, in their common efforts to relieve human suffering and distress. With heart speaking to heart, the walls which separate us can come tumbling down.

In fairness to the knights this was different language from earlier hierarchy messages about the Masons, the YMCA and other non-Church groups during a defensive previous period.

Supreme Knight McDevitt conceded at the 1965 convention that the hour might be at hand to allow wives to attend various "nondegree ceremonials" from which they had always been excluded, but he protested in a May, 1965, Pittsburgh speech that the K of C was not "outdated or obsolescent." Objecting to many of the demands for change during the final year of Vatican II, he said:

> Some writers and pseudo-authorities to the contrary, there can be no change in those matters which the Church has previously proclaimed as true whether by solemn definition or by the universal teaching of our popes and bishops. . . .
>
> Our own fraternity of the Knights of Columbus have not been without the over-zealous appraisal of some of these ecumenical authorities. . . .

Whatever adjustments might be made, the supreme knight said, the insurance phase of the operation would be continued and "only foolishness would abandon as obsolete" certain "forms and procedures" developed in the course of "the history of our society."

At the K of C headquarters some worker complaints were overcome by an agreement with the Office Employes International Union of the American Federation of Labor–Congress of Industrial Organizations, providing for a pension plan paid entirely by the K of C. Earlier employe contributions were refunded.[2]

The sort of changes which might be possible were suggested soon after the 1965 convention by Patrick F. Gorman, overseer of the 20,000 Knights of Columbus and 56 K of C councils in the eastern two thirds of Long Island, just outside New York City. He said that the K of C, the American Legion and similar groups each had been "going our own way, and really going nowhere." He said he would ask the others to join in united ventures "such as Christmas and Good Friday programs, movies and the campaign against indecent literature."[3] At least the outer walls of social segregation were tumbling. A positive step toward this end was taken in August, 1966, when the K of C voted a $35,000 yearly grant for support of the interracial and interreligious John La Farge Institute.

Knight Gorman's reference to the drive against pornography was no accident, for the old-line American Catholic organizations and individuals, in the final half of the twentieth century, continued to emphasize negatives far out of proportion to support for more difficult creative and positive programs. I asked Thomas J. Blee, of Fort Wayne, Indiana, national public relations chairman for Citizens for Decent Literature (an anti-smut group), for instance, whether his was a Catholic initiative. He said that it was not, in the sense that all faiths and none were equally welcome, and also in light of the fact that it was generally accepted that no single church could impose a successful program. He added, however: "It is a fact that the key people in our organization are predominantly Catholic men. This applies to Charley Keating [founder, and president]; to Dr. [Donald G.] Cortum of California and Dr. [William P.] Riley of New York, national co-chairmen; to Ed Rekruciak [chief of the Chicago chapter, and executive vice-chairman]; Ed Dahm [leader in Fort Wayne, and executive vice-chairman]; Jim Clancy, legal counsel; Ray Gauer, national executive secretary, and myself."[4]

Jewish and Protestant rabbis, ministers and groups had helped, but, Mr. Blee added, "our greatest response has been from the Catholic population," and "many active CDL chapters have been. . . formed with the nucleus of the local Holy Name Society."

The CDL and the K of C exchanged speakers at their national meetings in the middle sixties, and the K of C sweetened their reception of Mr. Keating by giving him a check for $15,000 for his work, and by asking all 5,000 councils to subscribe to *The National Decency Reporter.*

Both the K of C and the CDL emphasized that they were not only against nudist, sadistic, homosexual and otherwise perverted publications and films, but also in favor of constructive "good" work in each field. The emphasis inevitably concentrated on the rejection rather than the affirmation, however. The United States Supreme Court, a vigilant defender of the rights of American free men, conceded in the middle sixties that both the CDL and the K of C were on the right track in various of their protests against vile publications, but the sad fact remained that the old flag of repudiation once again had served as the rallying point for the lion's share of the social activity of a significant portion of American Catholic strength. A continuing question facing the American Catholic laity was whether mere negativism was contribution enough from a religious group making up one fourth of the American population.

A further question raised by Michael J. Kraus of Antioch College, Yellow Springs, Ohio, was whether a semantic revolution was needed inside American Catholicism, eliminating "martial language." He commented: "We would be listened to much more gladly if we put aside our combative rhetoric." He cited *"Knights* of Columbus," "superiors *general,"* the *"Legion* of Decency," and *"campaigns* and *crusades* for this and that."

"Is it any wonder," he inquired, "that the first reaction of secular society to this sort of thing is defensive, that Protestants break out into a chorus of 'A Mighty Fortress Is Our God?' *Aggiornamento* has not yet scratched the surface here."[5]

Both the Holy Name Society, the main American parish organization for men, and the Legion of Mary, a dedicated and often rather aggressive group of charitable and catechetical workers, bore the earmarks of what Mr. Kraus lamented. To criticize either of them, especially the Holy

Name Society, was to find fault with the very foundation of contemporary American lay mass spiritual activity. Yet these and other objections were leveled from many sides against these societies inherited from another age.

The Holy Name Society, with its American national headquarters in New York City, a stronghold of American Catholic conservatism, liked to trace its history seven centuries back to Pope Gregory X who, on September 20, 1274, asked the Dominicans to encourage the faithful to frequent the churches "with humility and devotion" and to "revere, in a particular manner, that name which is above all names . . . the name of Jesus Christ."

The Holy Name Societies as the United States has known them were born much more recently, however: in 1895, Father Charles McKenna, a Dominican, got permission from Rome to be dispensed from a 1604 Bull of Pope Clement VIII ("Quaecumque"). The seventeenth-century papal decree had limited confraternities and pious unions to one to a town. The dispensation meant that every parish could have a Holy Name Society. The spread of Father McKenna's organization after that was phenomenal. By 1907 there was support enough to warrant a publication, *The Holy Name Journal.* Men of many hundreds of parishes were encouraged to receive Communion in a body each month, and there were annual Communion breakfasts with jokes and a few serious talks. Many of the latter were on communism. Like the K of C, the Holy Name saw to it that meetings were "fun" as well as devout. Smokers, beer parties and the showing of sports films were part of the program. *This is Your Society,* a pamphlet circulated in the sixties by the New York national headquarters, had this further observation about "fun": "Perhaps the most characteristic [aspect] of the Diocesan Union of the Society is that it is engaged in a public profession of faith. Through parades, rallies, and outdoor demonstrations, the non-Catholic's attention is

183

brought to the Holy Name Society. In many cities monster parades are held in which thousands of men participate, and the impact on the non-Catholic must be impressive."

In a more ecumenical era one might wonder whether the adjective "oppressive" could be added as well. Some Holy Name diocesan groups evidently thought that "yes" was the answer to this question, for the June–July, 1965, issue of *Alert Catholic Men,* a publication of the bishops' National Council of Catholic Men, carried this item: "The Paterson, New Jersey, Holy Name Society cancelled the annual diocesan Holy Name Society parade. There is a growing sentiment that such parades have served their purpose. Other programs are now in order."

Norman A. Murdock, a speaker at the April, 1963, biennial convention of the National Council of Catholic Men held in Atlantic City, suggested that the name of the men's parish societies be changed. He argued: "I feel [the Holy Name title] is misleading. It gives no conception or meaning to the organization for the uninitiated, and has very little appeal to the Catholic layman of today. Maybe 'Council of Catholic Men' would [present] a more meaningful ideal."

Pope Gregory X and subsequent pontiffs to whom Father McKenna traced the earliest origins of his parish men's groups had been anxious to inhibit the blasphemous use of the name of Jesus and of God. That remained a Holy Name ideal though one of progressively fading importance as a working-class Catholic population moved upward from a world of gutter talk.

Another speaker at the same 1963 convention of the NCCM, the Very Reverend Monsignor John J. Egan, made a much more important criticism of the main spiritual organization of American Catholic laymen. He said:

The typical men's parish society was founded for one of four purposes:

1. To encourage men to receive Holy Communion at least once a month,

2. To provide beneficial entertainment and sometimes a spiritual homily in the pre-television era,

3. To insulate the men of the parish against unnecessary social contacts with non-Catholics, and

4. To raise money.

As Monsignor Egan pointed out, number three was not only dated but harmful in an age when Vatican II had asked laymen to be the bearers of Christian values inside an evolving civilization. The parish society, and one could read "Holy Name," which wanted to meet the challenges of the final twentieth-century decades would, said the monsignor, have to "recognize frankly that its roots are in an older world, and must work consciously to eradicate them."

The fifty-eight-year-old *Holy Name Journal* died quietly in 1966, and was replaced by a six-page "Holy Name Newsletter" dedicated to the reporting of new ideas for the venerable medium of American Catholic lay spiritual activity.[6]

The Legion of Mary, another of the Church organizations with faint martial overtones deplored by Antioch's Mr. Kraus, was founded in 1921 by Frank Duff, an Irishman. Organization was quite military. The standard beside which members renewed fealty each year to "Mary, queen of the legion" was reminiscent of the one used by Caesar's soldiers and, indeed, bore a Latin inscription: *Legio Mariae,* Mary's legion. Persecution in Red China gave the legion martyrs, and a long list of charitable works (visits to jails, hospitals, insane asylums) won praise from pastors as a practical expression of brotherly love.

The Legion of Mary could not be criticized for squandering members' time on social activities little needed inside a merged plural community, but it showed small appeal for most Catholic men. One of the few full-time diocesan spiritual directors of the Legion of Mary, Father William J. McCarren, of Brooklyn, said in *The Tablet* on March 10, 1966, that it was his theory that the problem never would be overcome until all-male units or "praesidia" of the legion were founded. "History," he said, "has branded the Legion as a woman's group. In fact in some circles even most women [refuse] to join it because 'it's only for old hens and gossips and maybe some men who are old or suspect.' "

James J. Wallace, the Brooklyn diocesan president of the legion, agreed in the same issue of *The Tablet* with Father McCarren. He protested: "It always angers me when I hear the Legion of Mary referred to as a weak, sissy organization for old ladies."

Another of the veteran organizations competing for lay support was the St. Vincent de Paul Society. It, too, had practiced Christianity in a concrete way among those who were most needy. It was founded in 1833 in Paris by a twenty-year-old student at the Paris Law School, Frederic Ozanam, who had been shocked by contemporaries who told him that Christianity, a once valid theory of society, had dried out and died. They challenged him to show what practical good was accomplished by believers in Christ. He and a small group of students of the same young age set out to disprove the critics. As in the case of the inspirations of Fathers Mc-Givney and McKenna and of Frank Duff, the early response to the efforts of the young laymen were phenomenal. By 1845 the pope recognized Ozanam's "St. Vincent de Paul Society" with several indulgences—pledges of grace for the French-man's collaborators. A year later the new society crossed the Atlantic to the United States. By 1951 there were 205,000 members in 17,000 "conferences" or mercy teams around the world, 6,000 of them in the Western Hemisphere. The 1965 count of St. Vincent de Paul Society units inside the United States was 4,500.[7]

A pamphlet of the St. Vincent de Paul Society distributed

in the sixties by the American national headquarters in New York provided this report on a typical large Vincentian grouping:

Members of the two-person teams which distribute charity and seek to bring lapsed Catholics back to the Sacraments of penance and communion: 1,087.

Vincentians who give financial support alone: 400.

Funds dropped into the society's "secret bag" by members of the two-person teams: $10,788 in one year, or about $10 each.

Funds given by wellwishers: $516,683 in a year. Visits to distribute cash, clothing and other gifts, and to offer spiritual help: 118,913 in a year (with an average of about four dollars in bills left during each call).

James Norris, an employe of the American Catholic bishops' world charity organization, and the first layman allowed to present a resolution to an ecumenical council (Vatican II, where he asked for a new Holy See section to encourage international aid), cited the St. Vincent de Paul workers to me as the laymen he most admired. Ozanam's vision of concrete works of mercy was still having happy effects.

But the St. Vincent de Paul Society, like many of the other old-time Catholic lay organizations, was in difficulty. Dennis Clark, a speaker at the 1963 Atlantic City convention of the National Council of Catholic Men, pointed out that all too many Catholic lay organizations had grown tired, keeping old officers and old ways, and doing nothing to draw youth. He said: "A few years back, the Superior General of the Society of St. Vincent de Paul addressed the universal congress of his brothers with this remark:

" 'Your besetting sin is senescence. In origin, in the Confraternity of St. Vincent de Paul, none were over twenty-two. See the average age here now—sixty?' "

An error of the Ozanam society, at least where the second half of the twentieth century in the United States was concerned, may have been underlined unwittingly in one official publication of the national headquarters. It pointed out that in a typical case the parish pastor would appoint the conference president for life, and cited what the pamphlet author considered a possible reply from a grateful unit member: "It is a pleasure to know that we are not to be bothered every year with the disturbing task of holding elections. Freedom from this annoyance will give our officers fuller opportunity to do their work without regard for popularity and creating artificial friendships."

Another sample "possible" comment from a charity recipient was this: "These Vincentians are charity-in-overalls. . . . Some of them, when they were kids, were twice as poor as I have ever been. . . . They had to put up with real poverty and hunger . . . and I guess that's . . . why they never had to go to college to learn how to treat [poverty and hunger]."

A lay organization without machinery for periodic renewal, and with expectation mainly of untutored "charity in overalls," perhaps had remained so loyal to details of Ozanam's original "Vincentian methods" that it failed to speak to the 1960s in the way in which the inspired law student had addressed the 1830s.

If negatives piled high on the one side, there were signs of vitality on the other. Much of this stemmed directly from the hierarchy. The National Council of Catholic Men and the National Council of Catholic Women, founded just after World War I by the American bishops, did an enlightened job in the sixties of wooing the laity outside the walls of the parish church into responsible participation in both the world and local communities. Martin Work for the men and Margaret Mealey for the women did such a remarkable job of preaching the one-world doctrine, as a matter of fact, that one corner of American laywoman Catholicism, the ladies of Cardinal McIntyre's highly conservative Los Angeles archdiocese, seceded. In an open letter to the National Council of Catholic Women, the Los Angeles chapter announced that it was reorganizing as an autonomous unit and gave as the reason:

The NCCW bias, slant and preoccupation with the United Nations, UNICEF, UNESCO, WHO and other specialized agencies of the UN. . . . [Also] the NCCW's omission to build up love of and pride in the United States, its clinging to citizenship-in-a-democracy versus citizenship-in-a-republic, its frowning on nationalism, and its paralleling the work of the Communists who foster nationalistic propaganda in other countries while they foster internationalism in the United States.[8]

The NCCM and the NCCW coordinated about 20,000 of the 100,000 American Catholic organizations as the sixties began.[9] A large share of the main Catholic groups were involved, but the man in the pew basically was a nonjoiner. Mr. Work estimated that only 25 percent of the Catholic laymen of the country were inscribed in NCCM member groups. By 1965 the NCCM was functioning in merely 60 percent of the country's dioceses. Although the Martin Work group was the official agency of the entire hierarchy, each diocese had autonomy and two fifths chose to do without the ecumenical and world-minded vision which NCCM and its sister organization provided.

The NCCM in the middle sixties was in the vanguard of Church spokesmen criticizing a wide range of Catholic organizations as "hollow shells," inward-looking groups alive merely for the sake of existing, wasting the time of the few busy parishioners who attended meetings, and continuing year after year with officers whose main recommendation was a dogged, unimaginative perseverance which had given them seniority if not vision.

Set against these groups which included a large share of parish organizations were a few relatively new movements operating on a national and even world basis. These offered a challenge to the educated laymen and responded to Vatican II's appeals for a lay contribution to the modern world. Because they existed there was hope that a significant American Catholic social, intellectual, moral and spiritual contribution would be made for the first time. Among these were:

The Christian Family Movement of Chicago, a group dedicated to the idea that the ancient tendency to separate the males and females was mistaken, and that husband and wife teams could be effective nuclei in sponsoring needed local swimming pools, arranging for chaperoned teen-age dances, fostering sympathy for foreign aid programs and, in general, encouraging man-in-the-street help for the solution of modern problems. I asked the "secretary couple," the all too cutely named Pat and Patty Crowley, to sum up the essence of the CFM and the aim of its scores of thousands of member couples. They replied in a co-signed letter that the bulk of Church organizational work in the past was designed, in their opinion, to recruit energies for internal Church programs. They added: "We feel the CFM is a training ground for lay people in the necessary work in the world today."[10]

Some bishops were reported as nervous about the CFM as too much involved in mundane problems. Some in the episcopacy showed little enthusiasm for the growth of the CFM in their areas. But through much of the Middle West and, indeed, around the world, the product of a casual 1943 Chicago laymen's bull session flourished. In early 1966 Mr. Crowley, a lawyer, and his wife, Patty, visited CFM-minded couples in forty-five countries and came back with a favorite story about a woman sympathizer, who was trying to create "a Christ-like home" even though her father had had eight wives and sixty children. In Chicago CFM took title to a

$10,000 three-story headquarters building shared by two other locally originated lay missionary groups, the Young Christian Students and the Young Christian Workers.

Living Room Dialogues. Like the CFM this, too, was home-oriented. The American bishops and the Protestant National Council of Churches were sponsors. The idea was for the neighborhood couples to meet and talk about common ideals, differences which needed to be recognized and understood, and joint projects which could make for happier communities.

The Catholic Interracial Councils. This writer's own experience with these goes back to 1937 in New York when Father John LaFarge, the Jesuit apostle of racial and interfaith good will, and his aide, George Hunton, a lawyer, asked me to give a few talks in downtown Manhattan and in Harlem about peace among the races. I did so although I wondered, two years after graduating from all-white and largely Irish-American Fordham College, whether there was something crackpot and un-Catholic about the interracial justice project. I remember one Harlem storefront where thirty Negro children stared blankly as I, a two-generations-removed son of Eire, suggested that the same acceptance which I sought in America belonged to them, too. With a strange turn of the wheel I was appalled in 1960 at a New York Catholic Interracial Council forum when a handsome Negress took the floor to defend the rape of white nuns in the Congo on the ground that "Negro women were never allowed to have their virtue, so it's our Negro turn to get back now!" Octogenarian Father LaFarge, tired from many struggles, looked on as chairman and said nothing.

Even as late as 1963, as Dennis Clark told the biennial convention of the NCCM in Atlantic City, only two of the fifty American Catholic interracial councils had full-time staff workers (New York and Chicago) and only another two had even part-time help (Eastern Long Island and Pittsburgh). In his speech Mr. Clark said he would be "extremely surprised if more than 15,000 Catholics out of more than 40 million belong to these councils."

Even those few were hampered by internal controversies. There were lively, often unreported debates inside the national governing board about whether appeals should be made over the heads of local bishops in Alabama or elsewhere when Negroes were denied admittance to seminaries (with conservative majorities resisting the idea of going past local hierarchies to Rome). In conservative Los Angeles the chancery objected to the use of the word "interracial" as somewhat subversive, and also against the word Catholic; "it did allow continued use of 'council.'" With the removal of the priest chaplain, the Los Angeles Catholic Interracial Council, a successful battler against California's antimiscegenation law, died.[11]

International Aid Groups. The organizations to train paid and unpaid volunteers for work in Latin America, in the Peace Corps throughout the world and in both Church-centered and general charitable organizations were invariably small, but each added its bit to the growing flow of lay missionaries dedicated to the aid of fellow men both within and beyond the American national borders.

The Grail was a good example of how much could be done by few. Founded in Holland in 1921, the organization was designed to make it possible for lay women, single and married alike, to take part in apostolic activity. By the middle sixties there were only 3,000 members, 1,000 of them in the United States; but in the intervening years the Grail members had pioneered in liturgical reforms and in the Catholic Biblical revival, they had brought technical aid to Indonesia, Uganda, Nigeria, Ghana, the United Arab Republic (Egypt), Mexico and Brazil, and they had worked in Negro settlement houses in American slums and with Dorothy Day's "Catholic Worker" movement. Eileen Schaeffler,

Brooklyn-born, and a social worker graduate of St. John's University, was serving as the first non-Dutch head of the Grail in North America when I interviewed her in 1966. By then the Grail had a 400-acre headquarters farm (dotted with eighteen buildings) called Grailville, in Loveland, Ohio. I asked Miss Schaeffler for a thumbnail report on the Grail. This was her answer: "At the core of the movement is a belief in the validity of the Christian experience as a basis of commitment and a source of hope for modern man in his search for unity, meaning and happiness."

No better reason for any lay organizational activity or indeed for Church membership could be given.

TWELVE

Layman, Bishop and Pope

"Extra omnes, everyone out."

Scores of laymen and clergy who had looked on while Mass was celebrated for the two thousand "fathers" of the ecumenical council filed down from the stands under Michelangelo's dome in St. Peter's Basilica, and final preparations for another session of Vatican Council II began.

The majority of the nonparticipants left, but not all. And in that fact was symbolized the change in Catholicism which is presenting the laity with its broadest challenge in centuries. Even at an ecumenical council, the Church's supreme legislative assembly, the hierarchy no longer meets alone. The layman's rights and duties in helping determine and carry out God's will are recognized more fully than at any time since the Protestant Reformation.

As most of the others departed I stayed behind on that bright October day of 1965 as one of the one hundred permitted outsiders. Something over half were Protestant and Orthodox observers. About a third were Catholic laymen, priests and nuns, admitted as "auditors." The rest, such as I, were newspapermen and others allowed in for a single day. Voting began. The council was entering its final hours. I walked out of the spectators' tribune. In those relaxed moments just before the conclusion of the council the Swiss Guards, usually alert to keep everyone inside narrow areas, paid no attention. With a white-haired friend whom I met on my stroll I toured Vatican II's astonishing coffee bars, something few but members of the hierarchy ever saw. A word about them and that morning's guide should be introduced as a symbol of the layman's new role inside the Catholic Church's highest councils.

The council had three bars, one of them inside the sacristy and thus outside the building line of St. Peter's (connected to the basilica by a covered bridge). The other two were in St. Peter's itself, fitted behind chapels on either side of the long apse. The one in the sacristy served coffee, buns and alcoholic spirits and was known as "Bar-None," for non-bishops were admitted there. The other two, in the basilica, were for the hierarchy alone, and for such occasional wanderers and exceptions as we. The larger and more popular was named by Biblical punsters the "Bar-Jonah." The other, designated in a weaker punning effort, was the "Bar-Rabbas."

Inside the Bar-Jonah, I found a sea of episcopal purple. My guide was the only other layman present. Only coffee, cakes, sandwiches and soft drinks were offered. I was startled by three eminently practical but, one would think, unnecessary signs: "No smoking, please," a firmer "No spitting," and "Drink Coca-Cola for the pause that refreshes." Former U.S. Postmaster General James A. Farley, chairman of the Coca-Cola Export Corporation, was famous for friends in all places, and especially in his own Catholic circles, but St. Peter's was one place I would have expected his tireless promotional efforts to have failed.

Next to the "Bar-Rabbas," a structure like an American

Navy quonset hut housed up-to-the-minute calculating machines which were tabulating the bishops' votes in instants. It was hard to imagine a greater contrast with the council meeting: a conference, ancient in its ways, where no debating was allowed, and where speeches had to be prepared in Latin days before the orator stepped to the microphone.

My guide was James Norris, of Rumson, New Jersey, a layman in his late fifties, father of four boys, who was the only member of the laity ever allowed to propose a resolution to an ecumenical council. He recommended in that speech that the Vatican form a new department to publicize the miseries of Africa, Asia and Latin America, and to spur and coordinate Catholic relief efforts.

When Pope John's ecumenical council began in 1962 not even the eldest churchmen could remember the previous council. It had ended ninety-two years earlier. Even the Vatican archives contained little information about the rules and regulations of 1870 and hardly anything about the sixteenth-century council at Trent, the penultimate in the sixteen-century series. One thing was clear, however. Neither Protestants nor Catholic laity attended either council and thus, presumably, should not have been present at this one. That at least is the way minds often work in Rome. Negatives and omissions create their own traditions. But Pope John, a man with faith in his own humble instincts, thought otherwise. He invited Protestants and capped that by asking a lay friend from his Paris nuncio days, Professor Jean Guitton, to join the onlookers. M. Guitton, a Sorbonne philosopher, and a veteran of a half-century of interfaith peace efforts with Protestants, was the first member of the Catholic laity in centuries to attend a council, but by the end of 1965 he was joined by thirty other representatives of the nonepiscopal ranks including nuns and laywomen, several from the United States. In the front rank of the American lay delegation was James Norris.

Jim Norris reached conciliar eminence by an unlikely path. He took a commercial rather than an academic course in high school and found on graduation that he could not enter the Catholic University in Washington because he lacked three essentials. His four years of Spanish were no substitute for at least some knowledge of Latin. He needed algebra and geometry too. He enrolled for all three in a high school freshman class. Jim practiced so hard at the Latin, reciting it aloud at night, that when the need came, decades later, he was able to read his council speech, as prescribed, in the dead Roman tongue.

Jim Norris attended the Fordham School of Social Service in New York and then went to work for a telephone company. Assured earnings and relatively uninteresting work seemed to stretch out before him. Then came the critical accident of a lifetime. Monsignor Patrick L. O'Boyle, the future archbishop of Washington, asked Jim to bring his social welfare training to a mission (named for the Immaculate Virgin) the clergyman was running on New York's Staten Island. Jim agreed. Monsignor O'Boyle went on to become executive director of American Catholic relief in the ruined Europe of post-World War II, and Jim Norris accompanied him as an aide and as a successor in organizing American Catholic and then Vatican welfare measures for hundreds of thousands of needy on all continents. A one-year job stretched past two decades. The wiry Vatican monsignor, Giovanni Montini, with whom Jim Norris negotiated each step of the expanding program, became Paul VI. When the Pope named Jim to join Guitton and the others as lay auditors he smiled: "You see, Jim, I've made you a conciliar father!"

In the first months of Vatican II lay auditors were not allowed to receive Communion at the daily council Mass. When that barrier was lifted you could find Jim Norris and the National Council of Catholic Men's long, slim Martin

197

Work, both of them ex-officers of the American armed forces, behind a potted palm in the Bar-Jonah or the Bar-Rabbas each morning after Mass having a breakfast of coffee, cold bacon and hard-boiled eggs. They would heat the coffee in a pantry and eat the eggs and bacon from a bag carried from their hotels. The bars did not open until 11:00 A.M., and each was too hungry, after Communion, to wait. Thus "furtively," as *The Sign*'s correspondent Douglas Roche reported, a new era of lay participation at the top Church levels began. More dignified and reasonable arrangements for hungry lay apostles would have to wait for some other time.

Jim Norris and Martin Work, at the outset, were "auditors" in the sense that they were allowed to *listen* as bishops talked, but the foot inside the ecumenical council door opened greater opportunities for them. In addition to the handful of addresses which laymen were permitted to make during the four-year council, the two found that the bars were ideal for lobbying for the expanded lay role which both considered essential if Christianity was to have full impact on a troubled planet. Jim Norris was tapped for membership on council committees, writing the decrees on the "lay apostolate" and on the relationship of the Church to the problems of the contemporary world (the "13th schema" containing statements on nuclear warfare, birth control and other issues tormenting Catholic and other modern minds). Pat and Patty Crowley, of Chicago, the fairly liberal leaders of the Christian Family Movement, and thus spokesmen for what Catholic couples feel about the stern ancient ban on contraception, were others in Rome in the council's fading months, and again in 1966 as the papal commission of which they were members worked on restatement of Catholic attitudes toward family morality and birth limitations. I asked Jim Norris whether, as a layman, he was able to talk forcefully for changes in council texts at his committees' meetings.

"My experience," he said, "has been one of genuine participation even though we are only in the same status as that of the *periti* [the experts serving council fathers, almost all of them priests]. We are permitted to speak up freely at the meetings of the commissions of bishops, and we are invited to present written proposals on the various documents which are under preparation. In the interims between [council] sessions we are frequently consulted by bishops regarding interventions they plan to make, or on positions they should take."

Thus at least a few laymen had a say in the writing of the Vatican II statements which will serve as the foundation for Church "renewal" over coming decades.

I asked the Crowleys how they were picked and what they thought about birth spacing methods. In a letter on October 4, 1965, they answered:

With respect to our appointment . . . we have no idea of how this came about. . . . [We have been called] open-minded [on family limitation]. . . . We are grateful for this, and think we are open-minded in the sense that we think this subject needs wide exploration but also very thorough re-consideration. You will note in the recent issues of *ACT* [the publication of their family movement], the topic has been rather generally aired. This is a new angle because we had always felt that this was a subject reserved for the higher authorities. Now we get the feeling from letters that we must enter into it and try to convey to people the best thinking on the subject. We don't think this is in violation of the Pope's injunction [in the middle sixties] against theologians speculating on the matter. We think the laity (rather than the theologians) are doing it, and the CFM must take its part, always refraining from discussing or disclosing the context of our conferences in Rome. . . .

The sixty-person papal commission of which the Crowleys were part was made up of demographers, psychiatrists, medical doctors, and a wide range of others considered experts on family love and procreation. The pope made clear that he would decide whether nuances should be added to the traditional Catholic emphasis on sex as the mysterious and sacred instrument for new life, whether greater emphasis could be given to sexual contact as a foundation of happiness inside the married state, and whether there could be any modifications with regard to the use of such contraceptive agents as the "pill." Even so, the thought that a married couple from Illinois should be invited to Rome to advise Christ's Vicar on such a central problem of morals was a startling illustration of the laity's new tasks at the heart of the Catholic world.

The articles and letters in *ACT* to which the Crowleys referred included a few defenses for the old Church ban on contraception; but, in the middle sixties, accompanying these were a flood of laments about "rhythm," the one authorized form of nonconceptive sexual relations for Catholic married partners. Other Catholic publications joined *ACT* in the outcry. The articles and letters in a sense, for the first time, provided a new "teaching authority" inside Catholicism, a lay outburst bearing witness to a painful reality if not an insight into undiscovered moral truths. Typical items in the American Catholic press of the middle sixties were the following.

Article in *ACT* by Grant and Vivian Maxwell, August, 1965:

As we understand it the . . . "mind of the Church" is now open in this area of life. . . . We think CFMers have a particular obligation to [speak up on this]. . . . Why do only Catholics, by and large, hold that contraception violates the natural law? We suppose one reason is that Catholics have been taught the natural law as it is interpreted by one school of philosophy. Today we are re-examining these concepts and assessing new realities in an effort to see more clearly the moral laws written by God into our very being. . . .

Would permission to use contraceptives in marriage undermine our traditional position on pre-marital chastity . . . ? Why should it?

Is frequent and continued physical expression of love in marriage truly a necessity for the fostering and deepening of love, and for the good of the marriage? Yes, ordinarily. . . .

Are large or small families better? We don't think any general answer is possible. . . . We have seven living children and that's just fine by us, but we don't believe in any magic number. . . .

What about Catholic friends who practice contraception against the stated law of the Church? . . . We are convinced that this "stated law" is *not* the last, best word. . . . We hope for a change, especially for a change of emphasis. We hope the emerging consensus and future pronouncements will emphasize the ultimate responsibility of each couple to act according to Christian conscience. . . . We know personally a few Catholic couples who practice contraception now. . . . Without exception they are intelligent, dedicated Catholics . . They continue to sustain and develop their consciences within the communion of the Church. . . . They believe they must accept the final responsibility before God for family decisions including marital relations and family size. They believe this ultimate responsibility goes with the married state just as other ultimate responsibilities belong to those in other states of life.

Under the words of the Maxwells' placid prose was a revolutionary contraceptive thesis, and a rush of protesting letters in the next issue or two of *ACT* momentarily shifted the discussion back toward a more traditional balance. Publishing the article was a "blunder," wrote Father Frank Tobin of Chicago. "While we don't recommend a censor," suggested Vince and Rita Dwyer of Aurora, Colorado, in *ACT*'s October, 1965, issue, "we do believe you should use the services of a moral theologian . . . !"

Article by Mrs. Trudie Barreras, a student at Michigan State University (*ACT*, October, 1965):

At present our entire morality of marriage is a negative 11th commandment: thou shalt not commit contraception. . . . The thing to concentrate on henceforth . . . is the ideal of triumphant human living. . . . We have argued viciously that [contraception] is against the natural law because it is "artificial," a totally untenable argument in view of the fact that much of human existence is dependent upon, and enhanced by, mechanical aids, synthetics of all sorts, and so on. . . . Most couples are bored to nausea by the constant negative theology of marriage they've been fed: "it's only the second best state of life, and that only if it imitates as nearly as possible the celibate state or engages in fantastic bursts of procreativity." . . . Marriage is the best state of life for those called to it but only if it is lived to its fullest extent including the fullness of sexuality and creativity and spirituality. An asceticism which requires the utter negation of sexuality is not the proper asceticism for the married state.

A rancher from California wrote, in *Jubilee,* June, 1964: ". . . we have gotten married to be unmarried? Do you see why our non-Catholic friends believe we are all at the Mad Hatter's tea party?"

Bruce Cooper, Middlesborough, England, same issue of same magazine:

". . . I could be celibate now and find a complete interest in my work. I have even proposed to my wife that we sleep in separate rooms, or separate beds at least. She feels to do so would not be marriage. What I mean when I say that a priest's knowledge must inevitably be academic is that he does not have to lie in bed each night beside a woman he loves. A woman's nature is different from a man's. She wants gestures of protection, tenderness, warmth and affection, and can be satisfied with these. For a man to indulge in such actions can arouse deeper emotions and so he puts himself in a dilemma, so the logic is to remove all physical tenderness from marriage: cutting out sexual intercourse means cutting out mutual affection. Marriage can go astray.

Contributor to *The Catholic Reporter,* October 15, 1965:

Ten children in twelve years hardly seems like [the Church-approved rhythm method for child spacing] worked. It is pretty difficult to regulate one's feelings by a lousy calendar. . . . The

202

cost to our marriage was almost fatal. After a complete nervous breakdown, an attempted suicide and another breakdown we have nothing left to do but abstain except at the time of my period which runs on a 49-day and sometimes 50-day cycle.

Another letter writer in the same issue: "I think Rhythm is basically detrimental to a marriage. It's like saying because I love God I will not go to church. Because I love my wife I will not touch her. It is a double negative, a contradiction in terms."

Some priests, such as Monsignor Yzermans, the American hierarchy's spokesman in the middle sixties, thought that the lay lamentations against Church stands on birth control were a symptom of a deeper revolt against all Church authority. Laymen leading the apostolate of the nonclergy, such as Martin Work, felt sometimes "if we can ever get past this issue" that a new day of important service was dawning for the layman inside Catholicism. Taken either way it was evident that the mute man in the pew was finding his voice and was insisting on a hearing.

Some bishops were alarmed. There were many sermons in the middle sixties about the rights of the hierarchy and papacy as successors of the Apostles to lead the Catholic community.

"Those in authority," Father Andrew M. Greeley, the Chicago sociologist, reported in *America* on October 24, 1964, "feel alternately threatened and perplexed by the ferment they are encountering."

Several bishops objected forcefully. Bishop Loras T. Lane of Rockford, Illinois, the man chosen by the American hierarchy to supervise modernizations in the seminaries after Vatican II, had this to say in midsummer 1965 at the dedication of a convent:[1] "There are those who, contaminated by a rebellious spirit against authority, would leave all things to the individual conscience without any consideration for the means by which the conscience should be formed. Due reverence and respect for lawful authority is essential for the maintenance of just order and also for the preservation of freedom itself."

Bishop George J. Rehring, of Toledo, speaking in his diocese at almost the same moment, added these words:

[There is] a phenomenon of criticism whose proponents arouse wonderment, perplexity and dismay. . . .

All authority must be regarded as truly deriving from Almighty God, all authority therefore must be duly reverenced. It is bestowed by God because it is necessary for the execution of His eternal designs. . . . Its non-use in those situations which call for its use can cause Him only displeasure and offense. . . . Freedom likewise is a gift from God. . . . It must be used . . . [But] it should be clear to everyone who thinks straight that in matters affecting the common good, authority must be given precedence and freedom must yield to it. . . .

While Church authority defended rights which were traced back to Christ's mandate to the Apostles and to the first Pentecost, a democratic upsurge of the educated laity into diocesan, regional, national and even Vatican offices evidently was in the making. Diocese after diocese, slowly at first, summoned "little councils," imitating Pope John's and Pope Paul's Vatican II. Laymen in several sees in the United States and Canada were invited to elect delegates to talk over the main problems of parish and diocesan life. The laity were appointed to high chancery administrative positions (director of finances in the Chicago archdiocese, supervisor of real estate in Seattle, the public relations office in Fort Wayne, Indiana, the handling of community contacts in Miami, and even the office of diocesan executive secretary in Baton Rouge, Louisiana).

On the national level, even before Vatican II, Martin Work, James Norris and others were full-time professional Church employes serving with subdivisions of the National Catholic Welfare Conference, the "little Vatican" of American Catholicism in Washington, D.C., and in the Empire State Building in New York. There was still a "ceiling on upward mobility," as Father Joseph Fichter, the sociologist, reported in a confidential memorandum requested by the American hierarchy with regard to lay apostolate problems.[2] James Norris, as one example, had several priests, including even rather recent recruits, as his superiors in the NCWC relief organization. His selection as a Vatican II lay auditor resulted not from his professional Church work but because of another hat he wore as an officer of world Catholic aid efforts. At NCWC in 1966 he was merely *assistant executive director* of relief services while, in Geneva, he was *president* of the International Catholic Migration Commission.

A colleague of Jim Norris's in NCWC world aid work resigned to join a large American export organization.

"In NCWC as a layman," the man said, "I found it hard to get any suggestion taken seriously but now, even when I express a minority opinion, they talk about printing it and circulating it privately as another way of looking at the thing."

His new group was used to the democratic brainstorming technique, to a trial-and-error approach, rather than to the ecclesiastical pyramidal concept of decisions and orders from the top.

The practice of placing clergy in "both top positions" of most departments, as in such conservative chancery offices as that of New York's Cardinal Francis J. Spellman, meant that when jobs were available in United Nations social agencies Protestant laymen generally were tapped, James Norris reported. "They look around among the various Church organs," he said. "Laymen are in charge in Protestant groups but they are down at the third and fourth level in Catholic agencies. The Catholic laymen are passed over."

But was all this due for a change? In his paper for the hierarchy, Father Fichter objected to the layman's "low ceiling." He said: "This may be one of the reasons why we do not have a full exercise of responsibility on the part of the lay people: there is no place [in the Church] where they can have a real share of authority."

The physical side of conducting the Vatican court always included a few laymen such as Count Enrico Galeazzi, supervisor of the buildings and grounds of Vatican City. In the final weeks of Vatican II Pope Paul indicated that a share in the more significant moral functions might also be granted. He appointed the first five laymen, one of them an American (Dr. James Kritzeck, an Islam authority, of the Institute for Advanced Study, Princeton, New Jersey), to a new Vatican secretariat for relations with non-Christians. The five would serve, along with fifteen priests, as consultants.

The nominations were in line with suggestions various of the clergy had made. Cardinal John C. Heenan, of Westminster, London, had urged in the 1964 session of the ecumenical council that any new secretariat for the lay apostolate be staffed largely by laymen, and not just "old gentlemen loaded down with ecclesiastical honors, but also some of our young men and women who have to earn their living." Part of the Indian hierarchy echoed the same sentiments. Inside the pages of the American Catholic press, Father Ralph Gorman, editor of *The Sign,* used his June, 1965, editorial page to affirm: "If the pope sets up a Senate of bishops in Rome to advise him on the administration of the Church, we would like to see him set up a House of Representatives for the same purpose, made up of lay people, both men and women."

In the view of Douglas Roche, a layman associate editor of *The Sign,* the old pyramid of Church authority was disintegrating under Vatican II's teachings into a new geometric design: concentric circles with the pope and hierarchy at the center, but with all "the people of God," clergy and laity alike, recognized as baptized faithful and as outer circles sharing the same graces and destiny. The candid Monsignor Yzermans, who had a layman writing most of the press releases which he issued in the name of the American hierarchy in Washington, put the same concept a shade differently: "We have vertical authority now, and we will have to shift to the horizontal. There is no doubt we'll have a difficult period for ten or twenty years (until 1975 or 1985) with some bishops cracking down, and some people telling them to go to hell."

The right to make central decisions would, as seventy-five-year-old Bishop Rehring of Toledo anxiously insisted, remain in hierarchical hands inside a church which always thinks back to Peter and the Apostles. This was clear at the start of 1964 when the fifteen laymen on the executive board of the National Council of Catholic Men voted to authorize use of a four-part nationwide television series on the birth control controversy. The series was written by *Commonweal*'s sprightly John Leo, and narrated by Sheed and Ward's erudite Philip Scharper, who considered it an impartial report of the struggle between Augustinian severity and certain of the more liberal New Theologians. Archbishop O'Boyle and Archbishop Leo Binz of St. Paul, the two key prelates of the American hierarchy supervising lay organizations, disagreed with the fifteen and imposed a veto which was accepted without a public murmur. The right of the bishops to reject lay reasoning in an area of official Church activity was unchallenged.

But the bishops needed more than acquiescence from the laity. They needed lay counsel and initiative. Robert Hoyt's eyebrows were raised in disapproval on October 29, 1965, when he used the "Cry Pax" column in his weekly, *The Catholic Reporter,* to tell about the inscriptions on three new bells at the preparatory seminary in Wheeling, West Virginia.

The largest bell bore this legend:

> In memory of
> Most Reverend
> John J. Swint D.D.
> Archbishop-bishop
> Of Wheeling
> 1922–1962.

The middle-sized one said:

> In honor of
> The Zealous Clergy
> And Religious of the
> Diocese of Wheeling.

The baby bell, with its tinkly voice, concluded the paean:

> In honor of
> The devoted and
> Generous laity of the
> Diocese of Wheeling.

In the summer of 1965 I asked Bob Hoyt, as one of America's foremost Catholic lay editors, where he descried the line between hierarchical authority and lay initiative. He answered: "It's not a question that bothers me much, or rather it's not a question that I think can be answered in anything but a rather abstract and not-very-useful way. Everybody agrees there has been too much authority and too little initiative. How to make a change in this and how far the change should go are questions that need to be settled by practice and experience rather than by abstract formulations of which we already have a surplus. We could move a very long way in the direction of encouraging initiative and even sharing authority without threatening the ultimate authority of the pope and the college of bishops."

Old ways are altered only slowly. New Hampshire's democratic bishop, Ernest Primeau, toured half the parishes of his state in 1965 but found that only a few of the laity "had the guts" to call on him in the pastor's rectory to tell him frankly what they thought about their Church and its future.

Each bishop needed the oceans of knowledge and wisdom represented by the laity of his diocese. More and more would be drawn into diocesan advisory councils to counsel when sums running high into seven figures were invested in new high schools and when other major financial, sociological, political and even moral choices had to be made. Professor Albert C. Outler, a theologian of Southern Methodist University, an observer at Vatican II, summed it up in a talk at the 1965 biennial convention of the National Council of Catholic Men in Atlantic City. He said: "[Have you heard] that story running around Rome last fall about the bishop who had no *peritus* [expert counsellor]. . . . He explained that he would feel embarrassed to have a *peritus* much cleverer than he, and that after a diligent search he still hadn't found one that wasn't!"

Professor Outler added: "These experts, usually theologians, have provided the bishops with professional counsel and commentary, and sometimes with nicely-phrased Latin translations of their speeches. But normally they have not presumed to cross the border between *counsel* and *judgment.* This idea of the effective use of 'lay *periti*' might profitably work in a diocese or in a local parish. . . ."

Jim Norris, in the speech he gave at Vatican II by invitation of his old associate and friend, Pope Paul VI, did not go into detail about the new Vatican secretariat on world poverty which he proposed, but he did spell out the suggestion later in a memorandum to the Cardinal Secretary of State, Amleto Cicognani. Lay and clergy experts on international development techniques, he urged, should serve as a strategy commission for a small Rome staff headed by a cardinal from a "developing continent." An all-clerical organization, in Mr. Norris's view, was clearly an error. In early 1966 the Norris scheme was still only an idea, but history's logic was pressing for its adoption.

Laymen would occupy top advisory and administrative positions in the Vatican and in the diocesan chanceries just as they would inside the parishes; but Pittsburgh's progressive bishop, John J. Wright, made a wise point in an interview with Dean Donald McDonald of the Marquette School of Journalism in 1963.[3] Living a life imbued with Christ's noble ideals is the highest role to which any Church member, pope or layman, can aspire, he emphasized. He went on:

Would the incomparable place of the [martyred] Thomas More in the life of the Church have been enhanced had he been on the board of administrators of some English diocese in his day?

Would the beneficent influence of Frederic Ozanam [founder of the Society of St. Vincent de Paul] in the Church have been greater if the Archbishop of Paris had consulted him on the purchase of real estate?

Can you imagine discussing the place of the Blessed Virgin, a member of the laity by the way, in the life of the Church, in terms of her influence on the appointments made by the Apostles?

THIRTEEN

Birchite,
Catholic Worker,
or Neither

At the end of a lecture I gave on the Vatican one day in 1965 in northern Illinois, a mother came up to tell me her favorite Catholic story. Her folks on both sides for as far back as anyone could remember had been Protestant, and the children were being reared in the same tradition.

"My little boy came home from school one day. He said, 'Mom, we learned in history today how the pope sent *the Christians* to fight the Turks. Wasn't that like him! Why didn't he send *his own?*' "

The mother chuckled at her child's ignorance. "I explained to him," she told me, "that it's *the Jews* who aren't Christians!"

What the child did not know about 500 million Catholics being Christians was matched by the mother missing the fact that not just the few million Jews but 2 billion others around the planet—two thirds of humanity—were non-Christian.

A son of Mayflower stock in Vermont told me of his Congregationalist upbringing in the 1920s: "We were taught to fear God and to work hard," he said. "We didn't know much about others, and we didn't particularly care to learn. I remember once seeing a little colored boy brushing his teeth with X tooth paste. We never used that brand ourselves. For years afterward I thought that X was a special kind for Negroes."

In a new world of an exploding population and of shrinking distances, the 50 million Catholic laity of the United States and their 450 million lay co-religionists around the world faced a unique challenge following Vatican II. Council documents gave the laymen wide mandates to serve as the Church's main agents in carrying Christian principles into a divided, suspicious, hostile congeries of faiths, philosophies, races, classes and nations. There were broad valleys of ignorance and ill will to bridge. The mute layman in the pew, eager for an opportunity to speak up and to act, had a mission as expansive as the planet itself. The need for his labors was clear. Unhappily there was no sign in the late 1960s that the layman in general was willing or able to take up the mammoth burden.

What was the job?

To help America's neediest group, the 19 million Negroes, find a place in society fit for citizens and fellow humans.

To make contact with Protestants as brother Christians.

To embrace the Jew as a child of the same Old Testament tradition and as a member of an extraordinarily cultured and educated group.

To support the public school system as a key to the solution of central American problems and to go beyond that to full participation in such civic enterprises as the Community Chest.

To help the federal government with welfare efforts such as Operation Head Start for needy children of kindergarten age, the Job Corps for older persons and the Peace Corps for world aid.

To cooperate, if only as a voter, in efforts to help Red-threatened Latin America and to roll back world poverty and famine.

To engage in an intellectual dialogue with a nation and world which are progressively less concerned about theories of God and of spiritual values.

Was the average member of the Knights of Columbus or of the Altar Society ready for all of this or for any of it? Was he or she even convinced that any of these were proper objectives? Yards of texts of conciliar statements, papal encyclicals and speeches at conventions of the National Councils of Catholic Men and Women made clear that these were indeed the layman's objectives, but there was good reason to believe that a negative answer would have to be given for most laymen in answer to both questions.

Father Bernard Cooke, a Jesuit, made this appraisal for the National Council of Catholic Men in the middle sixties:

For the most part . . . history has caught us unprepared. We are not ready for the vision of Christianity that has come with Vatican II. . . . Unless really thorough and pertinent training is given lay Catholic leadership the talk about the new function of the layman in the Church will, for the most part, remain just that: talk that will not eventuate in effective activity.

John F. Donnelly, president of the NCCM, the central organization of American Catholic laymen, was of the same opinion when this writer asked for his comment. He replied:

We know in general . . . that the problems of race relations, education, good government, world peace and sound family life are all [areas] where the layman must bring the Christian witness to bear. . . . So far as the National Council of Catholic Men is concerned, I believe our primary role over the next few years is, by

213

working . . . with organizations, to help the layman see how it is he fulfills the heavy responsibilities outlined in (Vatican II's) "Constitution on the Church."

Nobody really sees how this is going to be made effective.[1]

One factor working against the emergence of the civic-minded layman was what Father J. Paul Carrico, film study director of the Niles, Illinois, Notre Dame High School for Boys, called the American Catholic "do-not culture." Writing in the Christian Family Movement's *ACT* for February, 1966, he pointed out the way in which the ghetto Catholic "gave up" candy, movies, smoking or alcohol as a Lenten penance, and how negatives served as the underpinning for the individual's whole religious life. He added: "One got the impression that the perfect man was one who did absolutely nothing. We [have] specialized in do-not penances. We [have] failed to understand that if a person worked out his destiny with a sense of dedication he would naturally face fierce penances without seeking any artificial ones."

Another drag was the extent to which laymen and even priests and bishops found it hard to measure up to the international and interracial ideals proposed by the popes. This writer listened with fascination to this exchange between Pope John XXIII and New York's keenly patriotic Cardinal Spellman just after John's election in 1958.

Pope John (in Italian) : "You Americans [accompanying the New York churchman] make great efforts to lead good Christian lives, but you must help the rest of the world generously."

Cardinal Spellman (translating) : "The Holy Father says . . . that 'we must help other countries,' and we certainly do!"

The pope understood some English. He beckoned to the cardinal and whispered.

Pope John: "I just told Cardinal Spellman that cardinals advise and it's the pope who makes the decisions."

Cardinal Spellman, flushed: "The Holy Father says that 'the pope decides,' and all of us know that."

As Monsignor John J. Egan, director of the Office of Urban Affairs of the Chicago Archdiocese, commented in the middle sixties: "[American Catholicism] has become as middle-class as most of its communicants."

American Catholic charity for the needy of other nations ran close to $200 million a year in the middle sixties but well over two thirds of it was government-paid. The federal authorities realized that the National Catholic Welfare Conference would see to it that each recipient learned that it was an American gift, something which rarely could be said about the huge government-to-government or United Nations–handled programs.

The actual cash bequest from American Catholics for world aid each year was only five million dollars in 1965, the same quota as for nineteen years earlier. West German Catholics, half as numerous, gave nearly five times as much. When the American national collection rose one or two million dollars over the national quota the tendency, according to NCWC studies, was for the extra sums to stay behind in parishes or in diocesan chancery offices for the myriad of local needs facing each pastor and bishop: new schools, new hospitals. The end result, as Bishop Fulton J. Sheen, American national collector for Catholic foreign missions, calculated, was that the typical American Catholic could estimate his yearly contribution to the Church's overseas work at about forty cents.

The gap between ideals and action was by no means a uniquely Catholic phenomenon, as Robert Theobold suggested in an address on February 15, 1966, at the annual conference of the Christian Education division of the (Protestant) National Council of Churches. He appealed for nationwide legislation for a family minimum income of $3,000 and said:

215

The Church, if it really began to preach the Gospel, would deeply disrupt established institutions, including its own bureaucratic structures.

There can be no doubt that truly relevant preaching and example would cut deeply into Church offerings as is already being seen in certain areas of the country where there has been a concentration on civil rights.

The Church if it is a meaningful force is a disruptive one in a society which does not provide meaningful standards of living for every human being.

The problem of how to preach the severely demanding ideals of the Gospel without alienating needed financial support was one shared by every denomination. When Gerard Sherry, the retiring editor of *The Georgia Bulletin* of the Atlanta archdiocese, remarked miserably that "one can count on one's fingers" the number of American Catholic diocesan papers which could be called truly free, Monsignor S. J. Adamo, editor of the aggressive and liberal Camden, New Jersey, *Catholic Star Herald,* pointed out in *America* that that meant that 90 percent of the Catholic press was a prisoner of pressures. "The miracle," he added, "is that Sherry can count free diocesan newspapers on any fingers at all. If certain laymen had their way they would have cut off all the fingers long ago."

He went on:

On more than one occasion Birchites have sought to pressure our archbishop into stifling or removing the present editors. Other laymen have refused to donate to diocesan campaigns because they didn't like editorials on the race question or the peace issue or urban redevelopment or growing unemployment in the midst of expanding profits. . . . A bishop wants to see his diocese progress peacefully. What does he gain by having a newspaper that upsets and unsettles influential persons. . . ?[2]

Anti-Semitism, racial feelings against Negroes, the desire of a newly arrived member of the middle class to be accepted as a good fellow and as no troublemaker, the struggle to advance economically, all these combined with inertia to keep the man in the pew from becoming the social reformer Vatican II asked him to be. The letters to the editor in the Catholic press left no doubt of this, if indeed any evidence were needed beyond one's experiences with his own parish, his own family or even with his own selfish and lazy instincts. An example (complete with its own version of spelling and punctuation) was a December 12, 1963, letter to *The Long Island Catholic:*

Dear Father,

Answer a few questions prior to a number of Catholics drop their faith.

We have just learned that the pope wants us all now to change all our teachings about the Jew's having put "Jesus Christ" to death by crucifying him. How much pressure has been brought on him by the Jews, to do this, and try to do away with all we have learned since we were little children and all of our forefathers likewise and I am no child, I'll be 70 soon . . .

Their Talmud and Pentateuch teaches how they should hate, violate women and children of Christians, swear falsely against us. . . .

Just let me interject here I have close relatives, a Jesuit, a Passionate and a Secular priest, as well as nuns in different orders including the cloisters. . . .

I'll die away from the Church if you shove this propaganda down my throat. . . .

Veritas Vincit, Bayshore, L.I., N.Y.

As the Latin signature suggested, "truth" did "win" in that case, for Father Daniel Hamilton, the question box director for the paper, provided a sizzling reply. Without bothering to point out that the "Passionist" order, named for Christ's agony, is not "passionate," he got to the heart of the matter. The Pentateuch, the first five books of the Bible, he pointed out, are as sacred to Christians as to Jews, and "to suggest that it contains the material mentioned . . . is blasphemous." The Talmud, too, contains no such "vicious recommendations."

And, came the topper, "if you can't shove this propaganda down your throat, don't make any pretense of being a Christian."

For each anti-Jewish reaction there was an anti-Negro one in tens of thousands of breasts. "White backlash" was the title *America* put on this signed, July 25, 1964, letter from a Detroit reader:

> I would appreciate a detailed analysis of just what is "manly" about a minority group (be they black, White, Catholic, Jewish, or Irish or what have you) who demand privileges but decline responsibility, who *force* their way into certain schools but refuse to become educated, who *force* their way into certain neighborhoods but refuse to comply with the standards of those neighborhoods, who can gripe about the social abuses heaped on them but are at the same time guilty, as a group, of the highest crime rate in the nation. I submit that Negroes . . . are in fact socially and psychologically inferior. . . .

No matter which phase of the Vatican-outlined social apostolate was chosen, the same resistance, in greater or less degree, was found. When Monsignor Yzermans, the hierarchy spokesman, passed a night in early 1966 in a rectory in Manchester, New Hampshire, an area of bitter Irish-French anti-Yankee memories, the old pastor remarked at breakfast: "I don't understand all this be-nice-to-the-Protestants. They were terrible to us for years. It's our turn to get back a bit."

Boston's cardinal, Richard Cushing, had a similar story which he recounted in *The Sign*.[3] As the anecdote ran, his predecessor, Cardinal William O'Connell, asked the rector of one of the least-spirited, most rundown rural parishes of the archdiocese how things were going.

"Badly, very badly, your eminence," was the answer. "But

then, thank God, the Protestant churches are doing worse."

Papal appeals for a sense of common humanity and repeated gestures of approval for the United Nations as the sole available instrument for world reconciliation fell on many deaf ears. As Father John Courtney Murray, the Jesuit philosopher and architect of much of Vatican II's religious liberty work, said in *Life* magazine in December, 1955: "A puzzling phenomenon in America is the hostility of many Catholics and the indifference of many more to the idea of an organized international community."

Yet for all the resistance, despite all the support over the years for "America First," for Senator Joseph McCarthy's unconcern about civil rights in his hunt for suspected Communists, for Father Charles Coughlin's class-rousing radio ventures into financial theorizing, and for the John Birch Society's willingness to use "fire" to fight communism's fire, the mobilizing of a lay social reform witness began.

One of the most convincing preachers of change was an English journalist, Barbara Ward (Lady Jackson), probably the most sought-after of all laywoman speakers. When Vatican II thought of breaking one more precedent and inviting history's first woman speaker to an ecumenical council, Barbara Ward's name was mentioned repeatedly. Before a decision was made on the lay person to introduce the council resolution on international charity, Jim Norris campaigned among the bishops to have Barbara Ward chosen for the assignment. She was not one of the laywoman auditors. Some of the latter made it clear that they would like to be the first to breach the male monopoly at the council microphone. Pope Paul solved the question by asking Barbara Ward's earnest supporter, Jim Norris, to do the job himself. The council platform was thus one of the few major Catholic podia which the English laywoman missed.

Barbara Ward's thesis was simple. There was real danger that Jesus's parable of the rich and poor man, of Dives and

Lazarus, would be acted out on a planetary level, with the 16 percent of nominal Christians who live beside the North Atlantic playing the part of the damned rich man, and the continents of South America, Africa and Asia representing the "beggar . . . full of sores" who asked in vain for the crumbs from Dives' table.

In speech after speech to the National Council of Catholic Women and to similar groups, the English lady drove home her thesis:

The population of the United States and Western Europe, largely Christian in name, and representing only a sixth of humanity, has 70 percent of the world's trade, investments and income (one trillion dollars a year).[4]

The United States alone in 1965 expanded its annual gross product of $630 billion by another $30 billion—a sum as great as the whole annual income of Africa, and half as large as all of Latin America's.

The Ward proposal was simple: The principle of "international taxation" should be accepted.[5] Each of the prospering North Atlantic nations, led by the United States, should give "a minimum of one percent of its national income" ($6.6 billion from the States in terms of 1965 earnings). Christians should put pressure on local congressmen and parliament members for such a tax and for such foreign aid. With power balanced delicately between Republicans and Democrats, Tories and Labor party members and their counterparts in Western Europe, the support of "only 15 percent of the Christian [voters]" would be enough to tip the scales.[6]

And if the Christians refused to agitate for such an unpopular expansion of tax burdens? If the United States felt, for instance, that even a proposed $3.4 billion foreign aid burden, heaped atop a $50 billion annual arms expenditure, was too much for the nation in the middle sixties? The

Ward answer was ready: "We live in the most catastrophically revolutionary age men have ever faced."[7] International aid given by the North Atlantic nations was less than one half of one percent of their income in 1965. A doubling of it would represent merely a quarter of the annual 4 percent expansion enjoyed by the West European–United States economies. The relative ease with which such an aid program could be supported was balanced by the desperate need of so much of the rest of the world. Between 1950 and 1970 a half billion would be added to the globe's population, most of it in areas where a minuscule sixty dollars was the annual individual income. With the rich getting richer, the poor poorer, and distances shorter, the sole likely alternative to a generous, humane and Christian program would be a situation among "two thirds of the human race [in which] the pressures of poverty, the pressures of suppressed ambition, and the pressures of sheer anger at the disproportion and injustices of the world [would] be more and more pressing and more and more inescapable." Red Chinese agents were at work in Latin America; an anti-North Atlantic spirit was mounting in the world. Perhaps neither of these considerations or any others would be enough to continue even a small annual United States $3.4 billion foreign aid program, but "one can still have one last hope—that [such people] will at this point abandon all talk of a Christian society."

The Ward words were harsh medicine, but Jim Norris thought so much of Miss Ward, a journalist on *The Economist* of London, that he asked her help on his council poverty speech. He used some of her statistics in it.

The centuries of alienation from the Protestant branch of Christianity began to fade into an unlamented past. In telling his story about the Catholic pastor whose sole comfort was Protestant misfortunes, Cardinal Cushing was quick to add that a new day, "thank God," had broken, and that

Catholics understood now that a decline in any religion is a loss for the whole community of those who keep faith in a Creator. He had another story to illustrate that. An Episcopalian minister decided to replace his delapidated church. The local Catholic pastor was a friend with whom he enjoyed discussing books. The minister went first to him for an offering.

"I don't know whether your canon law permits such contributions, however," he said.

The pastor pondered, and then wrote a hefty check. "You'll need this," he smiled, "to *tear down* the old one!"

Catholic publications in the middle sixties had words of grief about the 1415 Council of Constance which arranged to have John Hus, one of the earliest Protestant reformers, burned at the stake as a heretic.[8] They spoke well of Martin Luther and of Calvin as men with many true religious insights, men who had spoken up for needed reforms, and figures of history who deserved better than the ogreish caricatures penned through the centuries by Catholic writers. Cardinals, bishops, priests and laymen mounted podia and pulpits at Protestant and Jewish services, and Catholic sanctuaries and rostra (though not pulpits) were opened in return. I corresponded with Cardinal Cushing about it in 1965. He answered:

[There is] an amazing and wonderful concern on the part of Protestants [with regard to closer interfaith relations]. . . . I have spoken dozens of times in Protestant churches and Jewish synagogues, and have found great friendship and charity.

Union is still far, far distant. But great steps are being made.

With Jews too, antipathies rooted millennia in the past began, ever so slowly, to recede. In 1966 the National Council of Catholic Men distributed thousands of copies of a pamphlet[9] for leaders of lay groups across the country listing reasons why the dense Catholic and Jewish populations of

Boston, Providence, Hartford, New York, outer Long Island, Brooklyn, Newark, Trenton, Philadelphia, Buffalo, Pittsburgh, Cleveland, Detroit, Cincinnati, Chicago, Milwaukee, St. Louis, New Orleans, San Francisco and Los Angeles, should live in amity: "Studies point up" that the juvenile delinquency, crime and divorce rates are lower among Jews than non-Jews, and that alcoholism is almost totally absent.

The store Jews set by learning is reflected in "a survey of heads of households in 1959." Results among the three main groups were:

High school graduates: 61 percent of the Jews, 39 percent of the Protestants, 38 percent of the Catholics.
College graduates: 22 percent of the Jews, 8 percent of the Protestants, 7 percent of the Catholics.

Efforts of the NCCM leadership to combat visceral anti-Semitism were supported by incidents such as this: When the Center for the Study of Democratic Institutions organized a worldwide conference on Pope John XXIII's world peace encyclical *"Pacem in Terris*—Peace on Earth" in New York in the spring of 1965, many Catholics attended, the Catholic press used columns to report the proud event, and then Jewish and Protestant philanthropies had to dig into their funds to pay the lion's share of the bills.[10]

Even in the area of justice for fellow Americans of the Negro race there were signs of a stirring of the American Catholic lay conscience. The same could be said of the Catholic share in the traditional American struggle to protect civil rights for all beneath the country's flag. The National Councils of Catholic Men and Women and the Christian Family Movement distributed tens of thousands of leaflets and booklets in the middle sixties recommending that home visits be exchanged with Negro families, that the number of Negroes in parishes be doubled if possible, that Negroes be invited to move into all-white neighborhoods, that Negroes receive help in the hunt for schooling and better jobs, and that decades of prejudice be balanced now with at least some favoritism. But in no area was American Catholic witness weaker. To some extent there was the feeling that slavery and the problem of the Negro 10 percent of the United States were, in essence, nothing which the relatively recent Catholic immigration had caused. The American emphasis on the rights of the free individual stemmed in good part from another tradition, from Magna Carta, England and Protestant northern Europe. But the Catholic's duty to defend and propagate a system to which he owed so much, and to foster human rights enunciated by Vatican II, was no less evident.

The Catholic press once again was rife with illustrations of how far the layman had to go to achieve the council ideal. *The Sign* in 1964 published an article by Father Rollins E. Lambert, the first Negro to be ordained a priest in the Chicago archdiocese. He polled 115 of the country's 147 colored priests, and received 81 replies. All rated the reaction of white Catholic laymen as somewhere in the "favorable" to "enthusiastic" range, but there were disturbing negative notes: Twelve answered "yes" to the question of whether any persons ever had refused Communion or Confession or some other priestly service because of the cleric's color. One told of an incident in Indiana when a white priest refused to take him as a fill-in for an absent clergyman. Some reported color bars at the threshold of religious vocations. Father Lambert cited two cases: a convent superior who told a Negress that although her community was praying hard for new members they would limit themselves in her case to a prayer that "the Holy Spirit . . . guide her *somewhere* else." The second was "a parish school in Chicago where the Sisters dare not talk about religious vocations for girls, lest a colored girl should be attracted to their own order."

The black priests showed no bitterness, and they did say

that their Roman collars spared them indignities which their color otherwise could have been expected to bring them.

To James Norris, the papally chosen spokesman for the American Catholic layman and, indeed, for the broader range of the Catholic laity of the world, the word for the work of United States Catholic school graduates in the field of racial tolerance or even in that of interfaith efforts was "shabby."

The National Council of Catholic Women implied in a youth leadership training course in 1963 that it agreed. It said: "Many American leaders, including Catholics, have expressed disappointment with the lack of Catholic participation in movements to encourage integration. For example, there are the few Catholic Interracial Councils, the small number of Catholics in the National Association for the Advancement of Colored People, [the fact of] little Catholic cooperation in sit-ins and so forth."

Dr. Ralph Lane, Jr., chairman of the Department of Sociology at the Jesuits' University of San Francisco, offered a revealing insight into lay attitudes about the Negro in a speech on May 12, 1966, to the convention of the American and Canadian Catholic Press in his home city. He told of an analysis of the vote on the 1965 California constitutional amendment which, in effect, legalized permanent discrimination against Negroes in the sale of small homes. Although most bishops and sermons opposed the discrimination, the highest votes in favor of limiting Negro rights came from the areas of the most thriving parishes. A further sampling of lay attitudes, Dr. Lane added, was taken inside one unnamed archdiocese. Questionnaires were sent to 545 active Catholic parishioners. The laymen disagreed with their pastors on social issues point by point. They insisted on less racial integration, and more freedom in the area of birth control; fewer rights where others were concerned, and more where their own immediate interests were affected. It seemed either that religion served merely a "masochistic" function or that it was just a socially acceptable and insignificant holdover from another era, the professor reported.

It was no sanguine picture, yet efforts of editors and of leaders of national organizations promised a more enlightened day.

The fact, as Father Albert J. Nevins, editor of the *Maryknoll* magazine, commented in the mid-sixties is that there are "two mentalities which are certainly not convergent," that of the Church *magisterium* and that of the typical American Catholic layman. "My problem," he said, was the ever difficult one of trying "to reconcile them."

A solution, Thomas S. Klise suggested at the 1965 convention of the National Liturgical Council, might be a wholesale exodus of laymen from narrow Church organizations to broader community enterprises, exchanging "the Catholic Interracial Council for the NAACP, . . . the Legion of Mary for the non-sectarian settlement house in the ghetto, . . . the men's club [of the parish] for . . . the city planning board."

That assumed, however, that such laymen were already imbued with the broad views of Vatican II. In most cases, that was still an unreal assumption.

Negativist right-wing groups exerted a powerful attraction on Catholic laymen. As the NCCM said sadly in a 1962 leadership training course: "Statistical evidence would seem to support the theory that a proportionately large number of Catholics are prominent in movements advocating such things as stopping all foreign aid, getting out of the UN, abolishing the income tax, fighting most welfare legislation and so forth."

A few Catholics on the left such as Dorothy Day and her "Catholic Worker Movement" campaigned for pacifism and resistance to the draft, on the one hand, and practice of charity, a sort of "Christian Communism," on the other.

Approaching her seventies at the start of the century's final third, Dorothy Day shrugged off the appellation "Moscow Mary" and had the satisfaction of receiving awards from many organizations who acclaimed her as one of her generation's most dedicated exemplars of the ancient and often omitted Christian "works of mercy."

A few draft card burnings and especially the tragic UN self-incineration of Roger LaPorte, a young opponent of the American armed effort in Vietnam, convinced most Catholics that Dorothy Day's "Catholic Workers" were on the lunatic fringe, but no one could take from "Moscow Mary" that her odd collection of bums and idealists over the years had given the American laity such eminent thinkers and leaders as *Commonweal*'s James O'Gara; *The New York Times'* Catholic religion specialist John Cogley; the Peace Corps' Philippines director John Cort; J. F. Powers, the novelist; Michael Harrington, poverty's portrayer in *The Other America;* and Edward Marciniak, the director of the Chicago Commission on Human Relations.[11]

Somewhere in between Dorothy Day's pacifists and mercy workers, and the pugnacious John Birchers, stretched the mass of the American Catholic laity, those who, in everyday life, faced the central task: to convince the "secular humanist," Mr. Average American, that religious values were pertinent, that they were still helpful in the creation of a going society, that they were still useful as an explanation for life. In the middle sixties, however, the American Catholic layman had not begun that critical dialogue effectively even with himself.

Part IV

Conclusions

FOURTEEN

New Catholic

News reporters love scoops. This writer managed to win several journalism awards in the fall of 1965 with a big one: the revelation that Pope Paul VI would make the first trip to the Western Hemisphere any pontiff had undertaken.[1]

The scoop took nearly a year of digging, of talking to those who might have bits of information. But it was based on an assumption drawn from common knowledge. I was sure in late 1964 when Pope Paul followed up the first journey of a pontiff to the Middle Eastern Holy Lands,[2] with a trip to India (the first a pope ever had made to Asia),[3] that "a new Paul" was on Peter's throne. Popes generally choose a pontifical name because of something they admire about someone else who was so known. It seemed clear after the announcement of the second journey that a second Paul was roaming the highways of the world, seeking to preach Christ's message to populations who had never heard it or had rejected it. For generations popes have waited in the Vatican for men to come in pilgrimage. In the world of the late twentieth century, once-dominant Christianity had shriveled into such a feeble force at the planet's seats of power that the new pope evidently had decided to emulate

231

the tirelessly traveling Apostle of the Gentiles of nineteen centuries earlier.

My paper was pleased with the beat, and it was my assignment to ride round-trip in the pope's plane a month later when he flew to New York to make a peace appeal to the United Nations. On the Alitalia jet, inbound to New York, I managed another scoop. I was convinced that Pope Paul suffered from the isolation of the Vatican, of Catholicism and indeed of religion in a world where even the stars are reached now by man's ingenuity. I was certain that the same logic that was carrying the pontiff to the John F. Kennedy Airport in New York would take him to the unlikeliest corners of the globe. Over the Atlantic the pope came through our plane to give souvenir Vatican postage stamps and a bronze commemorative medal to each of us. I was sure that the gentle, sensitive prelate would give at least a one-word answer to any reasonably discreet question. I ruled out the explosive and probably undecided question of birth control, and then thought of a few alternatives:

"Would you be willing to go to England in 1967 for the consecration of the new Liverpool cathedral [the first visit of a pope to the land of traditional no-popery since the time of King Henry VIII and the birth of the independent Anglican Church]?

"Would you accept an invitation to Warsaw in the spring of 1966 for the celebration of the 1,000th anniversary of Christianity in Poland [the first penetration of a pope behind the Communist Iron Curtain]?

"Would you be willing to visit the Kremlin [the first journey of a pontiff to the center of Soviet Communist power]?"

I was sure that the answer would be "yes" to all three, but that an even more dramatic query would still get a newsy "yes" answer. I asked:

"Would you agree to visit Peking [land of Asiatic Communism, the world's most virulent]?"

232

The one-word reply, as I expected, made an eight-column banner headline in the paper next morning. It was:

"Certainly."

Whether any of the trips ever are made is not material. The important point is that Pope Paul feels that those who have faith in God, specifically his own Catholics, must live their creed in the midst of fellowmen. In his view they cannot stay cooped inside the Vatican or the parishes. They must practice the virtues of their faith in the streets, preaching at least by example if not by word. In his concept, religion—precisely Catholicism—must try to convert the world.

To achieve that objective, far more than papal travels are necessary. The few hundreds of thousands of priests, nuns and brothers are also too few. The 550 million American Catholic laymen, as a minimum, must be enrolled in the effort. The gap between the need, as the scholarly Pope Paul sees it in Rome, and the reality, as any Catholic layman or believing person of any faith can observe it by looking into his own heart, is pathetically broad, but two facts were evident in the late sixties:

1. The Catholic Church which, for so long, had given secondary status to the unspeaking man in the pew, was on the verge of transferring vast shares of the Church's responsibilities, authority and dignity to lay shoulders.
2. The fundamentally unwilling and unready man on the kneelers of the parish church, especially in the United States, was about to measure up to the role of apostle in a secular world in an effective way which would surprise even him.

The $2 billion or $3 billion a year which American Catholicism had been spending for decades on education alone had begun to produce laymen who would take their place in the press, on the stage, in politics, on public school boards, in business, bringing with them at least the rudiments of the values taught in the papal social encyclicals of the past century.

The same laymen, locked away so long in their Knights of Columbus councils, in the Holy Name Society, in the St. Vincent de Paul Society, would start taking a lively interest in community affairs, in professional societies, in voters' groups. The Protestant church down the street, the synagogue around the corner, would begin to receive feelers from the same laymen, acting in their pastor's name and anxious to foster joint welfare and interracial efforts. It is not unlikely that on some distant tomorrow, with their Church's permission, the same lay apostles would ask for membership in the local Masonic lodge and for some sort of cooperative relationship with the Young Men's Christian Association, both of which were still out of bounds for Catholics in the middle sixties.

The possibility of a breakthrough in Catholic-Masonic relations was sketched by thoughtful Father John A. O'Brien in a talk[4] at the State Convention of the Scottish Rite Masons at French Lick, Indiana. He pointed out that the Church ban on Catholic membership in the Masons dated back many decades to France and Italy where various lodges, in the Holy See's view, had become centers of anticlericalism and of irreligion. By contrast, American Masonry "requires belief in God as a condition of membership," said Father O'Brien, and "far from being the enemy of religion is a mighty and powerful ally of religion." That brought the Notre Dame professor to his point: "[It is] unfortunate and pathological that Catholics, members of the largest religious body in the United States, may not be active members of the nation's largest fraternal organization." The priest, surely sensitive to the currents of new thought running through his Church, added his hope that a Catholic-Masonic commission could be set up soon to eliminate barriers to Catholic Masonry.

The "ecumenical" Catholic man was already becoming a familiar sight in the middle sixties, exchanging little-publicized church visits and even, as in Atlanta, Georgia, inviting clergymen of other faiths to sit, clad in their ceremonial robes, inside the sanctuaries of parish churches. But "pulpit swapping" was still discouraged. An occasional priest or layman mounted the preacher's stand in a non-Catholic church, but few if any non-Catholics and nonclergy were asked to speak in Catholic churches in return. Rome's view was that the pulpit of the Catholic church was for the doctrine of the papal church alone. That barrier to full communion remained.

The obstruction of centuries of separation and misunderstanding stood in the way, too, sometimes with comical consequences. Father Robert I. Gannon, a former president of Fordham University, one of the main Catholic educational centers of the world, was startled at a Southern banquet when the Protestant lady beside him asked kindly whether he was the only Jesuit in his family, or whether "your wife is a Jesuit too."

The necessarily celibate Father Gannon was so startled that his answer was sharply wry. "No," he said, despairing of much understanding, "my wife is not a Jesuit, but my mother is a monsignor!"

None of the normally portly males who make up the ranks of the monsignors was in earshot so that quip drifted into the cigar smoke and was lost.

A growing and effective role for the layman in the American Catholic Church is easy to predict both because of the shortages of religious vocations which multiply Church needs for the laity, and also because of the logic forcing the educated and affluent Catholic either to renounce his socially minded Church or to live its principles for more than the single Sunday Mass hour.

To make the forecast is not to suggest that the transformation of the man in the pew will come easily. As the Christian Family Movement of the Pat Crowleys and the hierarchy-created and hierarchy-directed National Councils of Catholic Men and Women grew in self-assurance and autonomy, and as the writers of the Catholic press flexed unused typing fingers, a tension between the clergy and the hierarchy on the one side, and the laymen on the other, was reported by many officers of the National Catholic Welfare Conference (the American Catholic Church secretariat) during the middle sixties. Old curates, pastors and bishops found the Edward Keatings, Michael Novaks, Robert Hoyts, John Leos and even, sometimes, the sensitively submissive Martin Works and James Norrises hard to take. They were not mute men in the pews. The line between authority and freedom was still embarrassingly fuzzy, despite efforts of Vatican II to mark sharply the large areas of lay independence and responsibility. As Bishop Primeau, of New Hampshire, warned his fellow fathers of Vatican II and as Donald Quinn, a layman, repeated at the 1963 convention of the National Council of Catholic Men, the line would have to be etched clearly or there would be "growing bitterness of laymen toward Church authority," there would be an increase in the number of the laity who would "passively observe the laws of the Church but take no part in her life and mission," and there would be "in some cases, unfortunately, even apostasy from the faith and from the Church."

"Leakage" of Catholics from their Church went on routinely by the scores of thousands each year as America's main religion—"secular humanism" as the Catholic clergy called it: nonreligion, agnosticism, even atheism, as it might better be described—continued to win converts. If, as some sociologists of religion did, you measured the number of the unchurched by counting all those who attended services fewer than four times a year, then at least half the American population, 100 million persons, had to be counted in the fold of the new nonreligion.

If you counted among the "secular humanists" all those who enjoyed the fruits of the affluent American society, all who thrilled at the opportunities opened by the science laboratories of the country, all who respected the leadership which "secular humanists" had given in the fight for inter-racial justice, inside the labor unions, on college faculties, in literature and, indeed, in every intellectual and social reform area, then there was a sense in which most suburban Catho-lics, most Catholics of the middle class, most Catholics in universities, indeed the whole of the American population of 200 million, could be included.

The problem here was to point out to the "secular hu-manist" mind that amidst all the startling achievements of a century of space travel, ancient questions about the origin and destiny of the universe and of man, eternal ponderings about the nature and purpose, if any, of human life, called profoundly for the traditional answers given by faith.

This in turn posed a double difficulty for the twentieth-century American Catholic scholar: to interpret ancient doc-trines in terms of the America of skyscrapers and super-highways, and to show that faith in some way had moved the 50 million American Catholics toward social and intellectual action worthy of a great inspiration. There is no doubt that in the middle sixties neither of these was easy. One of the troubles with the first was outlined in a frank and tormented letter to the Jesuits' *America* by C. G. Marxet, of Toronto.[5] He asked "what happens when the Catholic philosopher engages the articles of his faith in the arena of interpretative and critical reflection?"

He was not speaking of the doctrine of the Trinity, of three persons in the one God, or of the Incarnation, the act of God in taking on human flesh as Christ for, he said, those were "simply absurd" in human terms and had to be ac-cepted as faith's "mysteries." What he did speak of, he added, were the "large number of propositions" which were merely philosophical but to which the Church still demanded assent. He listed three: that the soul is spiritual, that natural reason can by itself, without faith, know that God exists, and that contraception violates natural moral law. Mr. Marxet added with distress and even a hint of bitterness:

This second realm of beliefs is the real scene of conflict, for the Catholic philosopher may well discover that the lived convictions of his reflective life are actually repugnant to certain teachings of his church, that his total experience is *not* a consistent whole. Then unless he can stomach the sacrifice of his professional and human integrity for the sake of religious orthodoxy he is forced to undertake a new assessment of the relation between faith and philosophy.

You can bet he won't receive much help on this fearsome project. It would be good to see a new word on this disturbing topic.

America made no comment.

With both the clerical and lay scholars struggling with modern reinterpretations of ancient faith, on the one hand, there was the question of Catholic social witness on the other. There was no doubt that the charitable economic vision shown by pontiffs from Leo XIII and Pius XI through Pius XII, John XXIII and Paul VI did not reach into every parish pew or diocesan chancery. In its August 15, 1964, issue, *America* commented perceptively: "There are some . . . of whom it could be said that they are so conservative that if they had been present at the Creation they would have voted for nothingness." The magazine insisted, however, that such foes of whatever reform were few.

How few was the number of those who clung to old ways, who followed the guide of Father DePauw's Catholic Traditionalist Movement, who deplored the "Protestantization" of Catholicism and much of the work of John XXIII and Vatican II, was debatable. Bishop Joseph P. Dougherty, of Yakima, Washington, thought the number was legion. He told a "leadership institute" of his diocese: "There is a slowness among the people in the Church. They do not want change. They are so conservative, and they do not want to be pushed. Because of this slowness we are not keeping pace with the speed of the modern world around us. If we don't change we will find ourselves more isolated from the world than we are now."[6]

Both resistance to reforms, on the one hand, and their inevitability, on the other, were clear in the late sixties. The pool of 50 million American Catholic laymen neither could be neglected by the few tens of thousands of bishops and clergy as the work of rethinking and preaching and practicing the faith went forward, nor could its volume fail of itself to carve out new riverbeds of Catholic lay intellectual and social activity inside America. By the late sixties some new forms were evident. At the Jesuit University of San Francisco, Father Eugene Zimmers began training a dozen or two lay theologians in ten-month courses each year, preparing them for work as leaders of parish convert forums. The program had mixed success. Hundreds became Catholic converts. One former seminarian, who had passed most of his adult life as a foot doctor, told me in his lay theologian office in a San Francisco parish that "neither my wife nor I ever have been happier." But I noticed with surprise that the ex-podiatrist's Sunday morning job was the parking of cars. In a little clerical world his role was among the lowliest, just above the janitor's. One or two of Father Zimmers' lay theologians quit because the pay was too low ($7,000 the first year, with a promise of a gradual rise to $12,000). Others returned to $30,000-a-year industrial jobs because "the nuns and the priests sat on us" and because experiences in struggling parishes were disillusioning: "They needed a teacher in the parochial school and gave the books and the job to a girl in the cafeteria; she wasn't even a college graduate. I'm putting my own children in the public school, and I've gone back to my old business."

An occasional writer in the Catholic press speculated in

the middle sixties about whether the ancient Catholic ban on marriage for the Latin clergy might one day be lifted. If that likelihood was remote, there was no doubt that the Western Hemisphere would soon see hundreds of married men in Chile, Brazil, Puerto Rico and other parts of Latin America giving Communion, presiding over Catholic marriages, baptizing, conducting funeral services, and even preaching from the pulpit. These would be fathers living with their growing families, but not technically "laymen," for they would make use of one of the decrees of Vatican II to be ordained as deacons. These would be married men with all the rights and duties of the priest except for the saying of Mass and the hearing of Confessions. Whether the married deacon might eventually become part of the United States Catholic picture in areas of a thin Church population such as in the South remained to be seen.

Whatever the future of Father Zimmers' lay theologian movement or of the married deacons, it was obvious that the layman's major role was not to be a "little priest" but rather to be himself, to be a "secular" American among secular Americans, bringing old Catholic moral and social values to a nation burdened and bewildered by taxes, arms and a sudden new world responsibility.

The lay Catholic in that role would emphasize what united him to fellow Americans, not what seemed to separate him. It was a safe bet in the late sixties that the type of organization which would *not* lead the new American Catholic lay witness in America was symbolized by a Norfolk, Connecticut, group, POLF (Parents of Large Families), which changed its name in 1966 to LFA (Large Families of America). POLF, or LFA, received a respectful hearing in one corner of the Catholic press as it told of the youngest children of large families who might have been birth controlled into oblivion (Herbert Lehman, Washington Irving, and Ambassador Arthur Goldberg, all of them the youngest of large families, Benjamin Franklin, fifteenth in a family of seventeen, Comedian Phil Silvers, youngest of eight, Jack Warner, the motion picture producer, last of twelve, actor Richard Burton, tiniest of thirteen). It had an audience, too, as it reported on history's most prolific mother: Mrs. Fedor Vassilet, a Russian, who had twenty-seven confinements, with sixteen pairs of twins, seven sets of triplets, and four groups of quadruplets for "a *grand* total of sixty-nine children!!!" POLF, or LFA, aspired not so much to campaign against *small* families as to foster the rights and well-being of big ones. But the day when Catholic and large families were synonymous was already fading in an era of "responsible parenthood" and of distress about the global population explosion.

The logic of the coming of age of the American Catholic was that the old day when Democratic ward heelers in big cities or Republican arch-conservatives in suburbs could "deliver" the one fourth of the electorate which was Catholic would be replaced by a new age in which something like the Christian Democratic movements of post–World War II France, West Germany and Italy would appear. John F. Kennedy, in a sense, was the first of this new generation of American Catholic Christian Democrats: sophisticated Americans sensitive to the need to defend civil liberties and dedicated to an ideal of interracial equity and of foreign aid rooted both in recent American and in Vatican tradition. The Catholic who moved into a proudly all-Protestant suburb in the Middle West and "proved" himself by raising a fund to buy out an incoming Jew, the Catholic on the Florida gold coast who damned the White House for inflationary, anti-Communist wars and foreign aid, and piously promised "prayers" to fellow yacht owners and cocktail party comrades, the millions who, through the decades, supported America First, Father Coughlin, Senator Joseph McCarthy and the aggressive and negativist John Birch Society—all these were remnants of a scantily educated, isolated, defensive past, and the result of a yet-unchanged present. But the John F. Kennedy whom hundreds of thousands of these deplored in 1960 as a nongraduate of Catholic higher education and as too much a liberal assuredly was the Catholic of much of the future.

Would the educated, informed American Catholic of to-morrow form a new party, a "Christian Democratic" and repressive grouping concerned with a "cleanup" of the press, of the films and of the stage, and unimpressed with Jewish and agnostic rights in pressing for aid to Catholic education and for worship inside public schools?

Some groups such as Protestants and Other Americans United for the Separation of Church and State voiced fears of such a trend in the middle sixties, but American Catholic appreciation of United States freedoms, the emphasis on liberty in Vatican II, and the example of John F. Kennedy as history's sole American Catholic president, were all powerful arguments that the constructive insights flowing from the Vatican since Leo XIII would win over the closed and reactionary ways of an unassimilated American Catholic immigrant experience. The days when Catholic clerical chancery "powerhouses" could play a role in choosing candi-dates for judgeships and for other political appointments were fading as a literate layman applied moral principles for himself in his own coping with political machines. The unlamented passing of the ecclesiastical powerhouse era was reflected in a talk which the Very Reverend Monsignor Richard H. J. Hanley, editor of the diocesan paper of suburban Long Island, gave at the 1963 convention of the National Council of Catholic Men. He said that "power-houses" did not reach men's hearts and were little better than useless. He commented:

During the past 350 years, the Church basically has had hardly any influence at all. [Papal social encyclicals?] I cannot show you any place in the real world where these things have effectively influenced society. Insofar as the Church in the United States is concerned I'd say that in this field [impact on men's minds] it is a non-influential church because about the only influence we have as Catholics here in America—this is a generalization which I am convinced has much, much substance—about the only real influence we have is not the influence of forming Christian consciences or putting Christian principles into the social, economic, cultural and political order, but about the only influence we have . . . is the influence of pressure and of power.

And the important thing here is that this is not the influence which is going to form the consciences of men, and make us a free church, a responsible church and a strong church of Christ in this country.

The new American Catholic layman, literate in the implications of his faith, and comfortable inside the free American civic scene, almost certainly would be called upon to:

Help his Church phase out some of the hospitals and charitable institutions which were founded in a ghetto era and could not compete or even fill a need in an age of immense governmental social investments, and of greatly increased operating and equipment costs.

Assist with an overhauling of the Catholic educational system, eliminating inefficient small schools, especially in the area of girls' colleges, and wedding Catholic and non-Catholic educational efforts (both through exchange arrangements with other institutions and through an expansion of the Newman apostolate at the non-Catholic colleges.)

Beyond the national borders the layman who once was satisfied with beer at the K of C or smokers under the auspices of the Holy Name will find a challenge in Latin America where the nominally Catholic population is rising at five times the increase in the priesthood,[7] or in Africa or in Asia where two thirds of the world's population is served by a tiny 3 to 5 percent of Catholic Church personnel.[8] Only the rare layman would respond to Church or governmental appeals for service as teachers, doctors or in other capacities inside the continents threatened by famine, by ignorance and by the appeal of communism and similar philosophies, but a thin brave stream of volunteers already was running in the late sixties as the fortunate fruit of generations of papal teaching.

The Vatican, too, was part of the future for some of the 50 million American Catholic laymen. Speeches at the ecumenical council of the early sixties insisted that laymen, too, as the overwhelming majority of Church membership, should have a role in policy making at the headquarters of the dominant Christian religion. The overwhelmingly Italian character of the Holy See was a consequence of geography as well as of history. It was sure to continue even though the Italian role inside ecumenical councils dwindled from 90 percent at the Council of Trent (the assembly of the anti-Protestant Counter-Reformation) to a mere 15 percent at Pope John's universal meeting (a conference which drew almost a third of its members from Asia, Africa and Oceania and nearly another third from the Western Hemisphere). There would be Italians in the papacy and in the bulk of Vatican offices for decades to come; but a rise in non-Italian representation would also occur, and the American share in that increase, given the wealth, numbers, education and organization of the American Catholics, would be just about as large as Americans chose it to be. When Americans— bishops, priests and laymen alike—saw the value of participating in global Church decisions in Rome, determinations affecting moral policies and attitudes inside legislatures, governments and populations around the world, that role, too, would open for the no longer negative, no longer ineffectual Catholic of America.

Notes

PART I—THE CATHOLIC YESTERDAY

Chapter One—Mute Man in the Pew

1. Eric John, editor, *The Popes* (New York: Hawthorn Books, 1964).
2. Christopher Dawson, *Progress and Religion* (New York: Image Book edition, 1960).
3. William Purdy in the *Clergy Review*, 1964.
4. G. Naidenoff, S.J., *The Catholic Church in World Affairs* (Notre Dame, Indiana: University of Notre Dame Press, 1954).

Chapter Two—American and Catholic

1. Monsignor John Tracy Ellis, *American Catholicism* (Chicago: The University of Chicago Press, 1956).
2. Gerald Shaughnessy, *Has the Immigrant Kept the Faith?* (New York, 1925).
3. Monsignor Edward P. McCarren in *America*, May 22, 1965: "We in the United States have 50 percent of the religious vocations and 47 percent of the seminarians in the entire Catholic world."
4. Ellis, *op. cit.*, p. 86.
5. *Ibid.*, pp. 47–48.
6. *The Works of the Right Honorable Edmund Burke*, 7th ed., Boston, 1881, IV, p. 305; quoted on p. 20, John Tracy Ellis, *American Catholicism.*
7. Article by Harry W. Flannery in *U.S. Catholic*, September, 1963.
8. Ellis, *op. cit.*, p. 44.
9. *Ibid.*, p. 45.
10. Monsignor John Tracy Ellis at the 32nd convention of the National Council of Catholic Women, Washington, D.C., November 11 to 14, 1964.

Chapter Three—Ghetto Catholic

1. *The Catholic Reporter* of Kansas City ran a Religious News Service article, January 28, 1966, mentioning that the John Birchite American Opinion Library distributed tickets to a Bensenville, Illinois, talk of Father De Pauw's at which 1,000 persons were present.
2. National Catholic Welfare Conference News Service, January, 1966. Father Welch pointed out that when Pope Pius XII discontinued the custom of fasting from midnight before receiving Communion, many Catholics were scandalized.

PART II—JOHN'S REVOLUTION

Chapter Four—The New Nun

1. Joan M. Lexau, *Convent Life* (New York: The Dial Press, 1964). Cited by Edward Wakin and Father Joseph F. Scheuer, two Fordham University teachers, in *The De-Romanization of the American Catholic Church* (New York: The Macmillan Co., 1966).
2. Religious News Service, October, 1964.
3. National Catholic Welfare Conference News Service, October, 1965.
4. Leo Cardinal Suenens, *The Nun in the World* (Westminster, Maryland: Newman, 1963).
5. Review of *The Nun in the World, Commonweal,* December 6, 1963.
6. Translation by National Council of Catholic Men, and National Council of Catholic Women.
7. Reported by the NCWC News Service.
8. Sister Bertrande Meyers, *Sisters for the 21st Century* (New York: Sheed & Ward, 1965).
9. Quoted by the Religious News Service, March, 1965.
10. *The Catholic Reporter,* January 7, 1966.
11. *Ibid.*
12. Erving Goffman, *Asylums* (New York: Doubleday Anchor, 1961).
13. *The Catholic Reporter,* February 4, 1966.

Chapter Five—Women in "Their Place"

1. *The Sign,* April 1965.
2. *The Long Island Catholic,* April 16, 1964.
3. *The Catholic Reporter,* January 7, 1966.
4. *The United Synagogue Review,* October, 1965.
5. Quoted in *The Catholic World* of March, 1965, which limited its comment to a dry variation on the old Latin prayer "Orate

fratres—pray, brethren!" Said *The Catholic World,* "Orate sorores —pray, sisters!"

Chapter Six—Gales through the Open Window

1. Genesis Chapter 7, Verse 19.
2. *The Catholic Reporter,* December 24, 1965.
3. Cardinal Shehan in a speech to the Serra International Organization on July 8, 1965, at Miami Beach, Florida.
4. Father Robert L. Richard in *America,* February 6, 1965.

Chapter Seven—The Crisis of the Clergy

1. Father David P. O'Neill, *Priestly Celibacy and Maturity* (New York: Sheed & Ward, 1965). Reviewed in *The Long Island Catholic,* February 17, 1966.
2. Speech before the National Council of Catholic Men, Atlantic City, April 24–28, 1963.

PART III—TOMORROW'S CATHOLIC AMERICANS

Chapter Eight—A Voice from the Pew

1. Quoted in *The Critic,* December, 1965.
2. *The Catholic Reporter,* October 8, 1965.
3. *America,* September 25, 1965.
4. Father Joseph H. Fichter, *Priest and People* (New York: Sheed & Ward, 1965).
5. Disclosed in a copyrighted exclusive article in the late fall of 1965 in the *St. Louis Review,* an official archdiocesan newspaper.

Chapter Nine—The Intellectual's Day

1. A review by Father Donald Zewe, S.J., in *The Long Island Catholic,* June 4, 1964, of John D. Donovan's *The Academic Man in the Catholic College* (New York: Sheed & Ward, 1964).
2. Industrial Relations Research Association, *A Decade of Industrial Relations Research: 1946–1956* (New York: Harper & Row, 1958).
3. The National Catholic Reporter, December 3, 1965.
4. *America,* March 13, 1965.
5. *America,* September 19, 1964.
6. *The Catholic Reporter,* January 21, 1966.
7. *America,* January 22, 1966.
8. In *Commonweal,* January 25, 1963. This was prior to the emergence of the Vincentian fathers' St. John's University, Brooklyn, with a registration of 13,000.
9. Catholics compose one fourth of the NYU student body of 40,000.

NOTES

Chapter Ten—Found: The Catholic Writers?

1. *The Catholic Reporter,* October 15, 1965.
2. *Ibid.,* December 3, 1965.
3. *Ibid.,* January 7, 1966.
4. *The National Catholic Reporter,* October 27, 1965.
5. *The Catholic Journalist,* March, 1963.
6. Quoted in *The Catholic Reporter,* February 4, 1966.
7. Edward M. Keating, *The Scandal of Silence* (New York: Random House, 1965) .
8. Martin E. Marty, John G. Deedy Jr., and David Silverman, *The Religious Press in America* (New York: Holt, Rinehart and Winston, 1963) . Reviewed by Robert Hoyt in *Commonweal,* January 24, 1964.
9. Reviewed in *Commonweal,* September 3, 1965.
10. *The Catholic News,* September 9, 1965.

Chapter Eleven—New Organizations and Old

1. *The Catholic Reporter,* April 29, 1966.
2. *The Long Island Catholic,* September 10, 1964.
3. *Ibid.,* October 21, 1965.
4. Letter of September 15, 1965.
5. *U.S. Catholic,* February, 1966.
6. *The Tablet,* March 10, 1966.
7. *Alert Catholic Men,* April, 1965.
8. *Commonweal,* July 10, 1964.
9. Article by Martin Work in *The Sign,* January, 1960.
10. Letter of September 13, 1965.
11. *Commonweal,* July 10, 1964.

Chapter Twelve—Layman, Bishop and Pope

1. The Mount St. Francis Provincial Motherhouse of the School Sisters of St. Francis, Rockford, Illinois.
2. *The Catholic Reporter,* December 17, 1965, summarizing an exclusive in the *St. Louis* (archdiocesan) *Review.*
3. Published in pamphlet form by the Center for the Study of Democratic Institutions, Santa Barbara, California.

Chapter Thirteen—Birchite, Catholic Worker, or Neither

1. Letter of September 7, 1965.
2. *America,* March 26, 1966.
3. *The Sign,* October, 1964.
4. Quoted in *Dominicana,* a Catholic theological quarterly, Washington, D.C.
5. Speech to the Catholic Inter-American Co-operation Program (CICOP) convention in Chicago, January, 1966.

6. From an article on Lady Jackson in *The Sign*, April, 1966.
7. From Barbara Ward's *Rich Nations and the Poor Nations* (New York: W. W. Norton & Co., 1962).
8. *America*, October 30, 1965.
9. *Jewish–Christian Dialogues* by Dr. Leonard Swidler and Rabbi Marc H. Tanenbaum.
10. The National Council of Catholic Men *Highlights*, July 1965, quoting the financial report of the Center for the Study of Democratic Institutions.
11. *U.S. Catholic*, March, 1966.

PART IV—CONCLUSIONS

Chapter Fourteen—New Catholic

1. New York *Herald Tribune*, September 8, 1965.
2. January, 1964.
3. December, 1964.
4. National Catholic Welfare Conference, June, 1966.
5. *America*, December 5, 1964.
6. *America*, September 21, 1963.
7. Reported by Cardinal Cushing in January 1964.
8. Estimate made in the middle 1960s by Archbishop D'Souza of India.

Index

INDEX

INDEX

A HAWTHORN BOOK